Be Safe,
Love Mom

Be Safe, Love Mom

A MILITARY MOM'S

STORIES OF COURAGE,

COMFORT, AND

SURVIVING LIFE

ON THE HOME FRONT

ELAINE LOWRY BRYE

WITH NAN GATEWOOD SATTER

PublicAffairs
New York

Hardcover published in 2015 in the United States by PublicAffairs™,
a Member of the Perseus Books Group

Paperback published in 2016 by PublicAffairs

PublicAffairs books are available at special discounts for bulk purchases in
the U.S. by corporations, institutions, and other organizations. For more
information, please contact the Special Markets Department at the Perseus
Books Group, 2300 Chestnut Street, Suite 200, Philadelphia, PA 19103, call
(800) 810-4145, ext. 5000, or e-mail special.markets@perseusbooks.com.

Book Design by Pauline Brown

Library of Congress Cataloging-in-Publication Data

Brye, Elaine Lowry.
    Be safe, love mom : a military mom's stories of courage, comfort, and
    surviving life on the home front / Elaine Lowry Brye with Nan Gatewood
    Satter.—First edition.

        pages   cm.

ISBN 978-1-61039-521-2 (hardback)—ISBN 978-1-61039-522-9
(electronic) 1. Families of military personnel—United States. 2. Mothers
of soldiers—United States. 3. Soldiers—Family relationships—
United States. 4. Military spouses—Family relationships—United
States. 5. United States—Armed Forces—Military life. I. Satter, Nan
Gatewood. II. Title. III. Title: Military mom's stories of courage, comfort,
and surviving life on the home front.

 U21.5.B76 2015

 355.1'20973—dc23

                                                                2014036598

ISBN: 978-1-61039-637-0 (paperback)

LSC-C

10 9 8 7 6 5 4

*Dedicated to my heroes—my mom and dad, my husband,
and my children, whose sacrifices of service before self
give me hope in a difficult world.*

ELB

*In memory of my father, who served his country piloting
his F6F Hellcat in the skies over the Pacific, and for
my mother, who continues to teach me about strength,
determination, and gratitude every day.*

NGS

Contents

CONTENTS

Author's Note

*B*e *Safe, Love Mom* includes information about my own experiences and those of other military mothers. These mothers have been most generous in granting me permission to share
their observations and stories in this book. I have changed most of
their names to protect their privacy and the privacy of their military
children.

With that same regard for privacy, I have, for the most part, kept
stories and mentions of my nephew, Luke, out of these pages. Luke
was an important part of our lively household for many years, and
we love him dearly. His story, perhaps, is one for another day.

My biological children have not been so lucky. In all cases, they
have been identified. Sorry kids.

Elaine Lowry Brye
September 2014

Introduction

It's the first time the six of us have been together in more than three years, and we are all giddy with excitement. My four uniformed children—Eric, Jordan, Katrina, and Brendan—are crammed together side by side on the cabin steps in preparation for a new family portrait, and they are laughing so hard that one of them has turned beet red and another is doubled over and holding his belly. Just like when they were little kids in the back seat of the car kicking and pinching each other, there's lots of physical contact. Except now, decades later, the punches in the arm, slaps on the back, and constant jostling are signs of affection rather than of squabbling. I close my eyes and am transported back to earlier days when they would tumble and wrestle together like a pile of puppies. "Somebody's going to start crying soon," I'd yell, and moments later, just as predicted, a tearful wail would rend the air.

Now, their hilarity interrupts my reverie. I am pulled onto the steps and teased mercilessly while my husband, Courtney, stands by, arms crossed, looking happy and proud.

In our family, connections of the heart are not expressed through long soulful gazes and earnest "I love you's." I know, and so would anyone watching, that all of the teasing and tussling of this joyous reunion weekend are expressions of my family's deepest love. And as my children press in next to me in their mottled camouflage—each uniform different, for each child serves in a different branch of the United States military—and their raucous rivalry escalates, I am in bliss.

The tangible reminder of this bliss—the latest treasured family portrait—will go on the staircase wall next to all of those happy images from my kids' childhood and teenage years—years when they were never too far from the nest; now, I glance down at their standard-issue boots and am amazed to realize that the dust of so many distant lands has been tracked all the way to the cabin we have rented here in rural Idaho. And on the days when having four children in the military seems to demand more strength than I possess, the love and delight radiating from this photo will strengthen my mother's heart and be my ammunition against despair. I need this photograph, this ammunition—oh, how I need it. Because I don't know when—or if—we will all be together again.

*A*lthough you and I most likely have never met, we have the privilege of sharing our child—or in some cases, children—with this great nation we live in. As they do their duty, we do ours. And sometimes it can be lonely here on the home front. Believe me, I know.

I know because I've spent a lifetime living with and loving those who serve our country. As the daughter of an Army colonel and the mother of four military officers, I know what it's like to have those you hold dear in harm's way. My husband is a former Air Force pilot, and I, too, have served. And now I have the perspective of someone who has lived in a war zone, even if not on active duty. From July of 2010 until May of 2011, I lived in Kabul and taught at an English-speaking school. It was a life-changing experience.

As a moderator of the US Naval Academy (USNA) Parents listserv* since 2001 and now a USNA Parents Facebook administrator, I have been supporting Naval Academy parents for almost a decade and a half. Over the years, my fellow moderators and I have answered the questions of thousands of parents who are anxious and worried when their child ships off to the Naval Academy, and beyond that, who are completely lost when it comes to having a child in the military. I have heard their concerns—concerns you may share, and that I have shared and in some cases still share—and I continue to consider it a privilege to meet these parents and to answer their questions and allay their fears. I have often learned about courage and duty and letting go the hard way, particularly as they relate to having children in the military, and if I can pave the way for you and save you a little pain, it would be my honor and pleasure to do so. Because we are related, you and I. We are bound together by our love of our children and their calling to serve.

I was born to be a military mom. It just took me a few decades to realize it.

---

* The USNA-Parents listserv and the USNA-Plebe-Parents listserv are two separate entities, and I met and communicated with people on both. I've tried to keep things simple by conflating references to them in the text, and so any mentions of "USNA-Parents listserv" might actually refer to either entity.

As the oldest of seven children, I spent a great deal of my adolescence proclaiming that I would never have children. "I've changed enough diapers and burped enough babies and wiped enough runny noses for a lifetime," I'd declare to anyone who even casually brought up the subject of motherhood. "I'm done with all that." Over time, love and biology made me reevaluate my teenage vow, and eventually I became a mom to four. My nephew later joined our brood for a grand total of five lively youngsters. All that early caregiving experience made motherhood a natural job for me.

And the military descriptor? I come by that naturally, too.

I am an Army brat, born at Fort Meade, Maryland. In my first eighteen years we moved seventeen times and I attended twelve different schools. Each of us seven kids was born in a different state. Watching the Miss America Pageant was, for us, a sibling competition—we each rooted for our birth state contestant. Growing up in an environment of ceaseless change meant that the only constant was family, which mostly meant my mom and siblings. Some years ago I added it up; my dad was gone for a total of seven years over the course of the turbulent Vietnam era, the backdrop for my childhood and adolescence.

By the time I was in my mid-twenties, I had married a handsome Air Force pilot named Courtney Brye, whom I'd met as a result of my own Air Force ROTC training. Courtney's childhood was the polar opposite of mine in terms of stability. He grew up on a farm that his grandfather had homesteaded in North Dakota—his mother, in fact, still lives on that farm—and he knew everyone within a ten-mile radius. After leaving the military, Courtney proposed that we raise our children on a farm, and I loved the idea of rooting our family in one place. We found our dream spot in eastern Ohio and settled in to tend to kids and cattle.

It's funny how things work out. We purchased a farm with the idea of providing stability for our children (not to mention all the lessons that farm life provides), and now, thirty years later, they are spread all over the country, and occasionally around the globe. They've all chosen to dedicate themselves to lives in the military, which for them means lives in perpetual motion, and for me means a return to my change-is-constant roots.

If you had told me as they were growing up that this is where we'd end up, I would have looked at you as if you were out of your mind. Our four children are very different, with distinctly individual personalities and ambitions. We never dreamed that three of them would attend the same college, the US Naval Academy. And we certainly never expected that all four would become commissioned officers.

It was not a stretch, though, to imagine that Eric, our oldest, might follow in his father's footsteps—or flight path—and become a military aviator. He soared over every hurdle in the USNA's admissions process, and when he stepped onto its campus in July of 2001, I found myself a military mother. It was vast, uncharted territory. I knew how to *be* a military kid, but to *have* a military kid was a completely different matter. As I began to grasp the degree to which I would have to let go of my son, I was overwhelmed with grief and anxiety.

Is it any wonder, then, that I quickly found myself exchanging dozens of e-mails a day with other new military parents via the USNA-Parents listserv? What began as a survival tool for my first summer as a military mom has developed into years of support for thousands of fellow military parents. First as an anxious plebe mother, then as a moderator of the listserv, and now as a blogger, speaker, and military parent Facebook page administrator, I have been privileged to meet some of the finest parents that walk this planet. Their dedication to their children, their unsung heroism, and their personal sacrifices inspire me every day. And I have also come to know their children, who I've watched develop into warriors and leaders of the highest order. I have heard stories of courage beyond comprehension, determination beyond description, and heroes made both at home and on the battlefield. Now, with four children in the military—all officers, one each in the Army, Navy, Air Force, and Marines—well, I have earned my stripes as a military mom. I grew up as a little girl saying goodbye to my father over and over again, and now as a mother I repeat this process in reverse, saying goodbye to my children time and time again.

It's just what we do, we military moms and family members, for our loved ones and for our country.

If we go all the way back to the beginning, even my birth had military roots. My parents met while they were both in the Army. My dad was eighteen when he was drafted during World War II. The first day of boot camp, someone called out, "If you want to be an officer, line up here." He did, and a few months later he was commissioned as a second lieutenant in the Army Signal Corps. It was an amazing outcome for a child abandoned by his mother during the difficult years of the Depression.

Who would have thought that that neglected boy would grow up to become one of the Army's youngest colonels ever, and on top of that, would not only complete his bachelor's and master's degrees but also earn a doctorate by the age of forty-five? That's my dad's story. His thirty-five years of service in the Army were filled with accomplishments, and a striking photograph of him hangs in the Officer Candidate School Hall of Fame at Fort Benning, Georgia. "Line up here" he certainly did.

I never realized the magnitude of what he accomplished until I saw it spelled out for me on his tombstone in Arlington National Cemetery. A veteran of three wars, he was awarded the Legion of Merit three times and received three Bronze Stars, as well; it's a story of valor chiseled into cold white marble. When I was a child, what he did meant frequent moves and frequent "tours" for dad—that's what deployments were called in those days. Now I see his service as his legacy. He was a warrior, literally and figuratively. There was a spark inside of him that was not extinguished no matter how dark the days were.

Then there was my mother. She, too, was a warrior, though an unlikely one. An industrial psychology major at Michigan State University, she was trying to decide what to do next when her advisor said, "If you really want to learn about people, join the Army." So she did, shocking her family and all who knew her. She entered the Women's Army Corps in August of 1952, and, after a grueling Officer Candidate School course, found herself commissioned as a first lieutenant and stationed at Fort Monmouth, New Jersey.

There she met my dad, and it must have been quite the whirlwind romance. After dating for six months they married in a civil ceremony, and soon thereafter he deployed to Turkey. A month after he returned from his twelve-month assignment, they had a church wedding. Eleven months later, I was born. In those days women were not allowed to be both pregnant and on active duty, so my first role was to provide my mom with an honorable discharge. I guess you could say I performed my military duty from the start.

Mom was the anchor. No matter where we were, she kept us all together. As a young child I understood that my dad was in the

Army, and I helped my mom iron his uniform, but it was a simple time and my understanding of it was simple. I still held on to the hope that my father, with some help and gentle encouragement, might someday become more like Mr. Cleaver on *Leave It to Beaver.*

As the sixties unfolded, I came to understand that this would never happen. My father began a series of tours to Vietnam, and somehow my mother balanced the concerns she must have had about him with the complexity of handling seven children on her own. I could tell she was worried, but rather than focus on her own pain, she started to write letters to the mothers of my dad's soldiers who were killed in action.

We moved and moved and moved. Whenever someone asked me where I was from, I answered "Michigan." Mind you, I had never lived there, but my mom was from the Upper Peninsula and I knew that *she* thought of it as home. And whenever a PCS—permanent change of station—took us anywhere in the general vicinity of Michigan, we found ourselves at our grandparents' cabin on Indian Lake. Those summer days spent rowing on the lake during the day and catching fireflies at night came to mean "home" in a world of transition. So my hometown was a town I never lived in—until my father's second deployment to Vietnam.

We had moved to Frankfurt, Germany, and it was supposed to be a three-year tour. I was in eighth grade and the prospect of the three years in one school was heaven, an unbelievable gift. But it was not meant to be. My father got promoted, which meant a new job, a new duty station, and another adjustment for the family. We moved to US Army Europe Headquarters in Heidelberg, Germany, where there were so many colonels that we didn't have a house to accommodate our nine-member family, but a three-bedroom apartment.

The Cold War was still on. We had to have the car half full of gas at all times, with evacuation bags packed and a route planned in case the Soviets crossed the border. But there were even more immediate dangers. At that time, groups of terrorists were attacking US military installations. Our housing was not enclosed, so we were instructed to be watchful. Danger did come, not in the form of terrorists, but antiwar protestors. Twice they marched and surrounded our military housing complex. I sat in my bird's nest of a room watching German riot police in full gear beat them back. On the streetcar, I could hear Germans muttering anti-American sentiments. My American tennis shoes and Levi's jeans were dead giveaways as to my origins, and so I began to dress like a German to avoid confrontation.

In the spring of 1970, I returned from a train trip to Frankfurt and was startled to see both my mother and father at the station to meet me. In fact, this is the only memory I have of being alone with the two of them during my entire childhood. When they said they were going to take me out for dessert, I knew that something was terribly wrong. And it was. My dad had received orders to return to Vietnam. We would have to move again—for the third time in eighteen months—and I would have to start yet another school. Worst of all, my dad would be going back to war. At fourteen, I understood what that meant. In my military-dependent high school, others had received news of the loss of a dad—few women served then—and quickly disappeared to grieve.

My parents had been wise to break the news to me in public. Had they told me in the privacy of our home I'm sure the vehemence of my response would have frightened my younger siblings. I felt like I'd been punched in the gut and stabbed in the heart, but while in the café, I held myself more or less together. Once home and in the safety of my room, I cried so hard and so long that my eyes wouldn't open the next day. I mourned the loss of my new friends, my position on the yearbook, the boy I had a crush on. I grieved for the small amount of stability I had established there. And I was afraid. I had a teenager's typical turbulent relationship with my dad. But now he would be gone, and something terrible could happen to him.

The next night I raged at my father, telling him that the war was meaningless and that I was tired of being a military kid. He told me about the Montagnard villagers he had helped during his first assignment in Vietnam, and how the people there wanted to be free like those of us in the United States. He told me that young men in his command were dying every day trying to keep communication lines open, and that he had a duty to be there to lead them. I called the president a warmonger who liked death. My father drew himself up and said, "You will not talk about the Commander in Chief in that manner. I have taken an oath to protect and defend my country against all enemies. I will follow orders."

And just like my father, we followed orders. While he shipped off to Vietnam, we moved to my mom's hometown of Manistique, on the shores of Lake Michigan. We were excited to be living near family—an opportunity we'd never had before. At the age of fifteen, I finally got to live in my very own hometown.

It was a difficult time to be a military family in a civilian community. The antiwar sentiment was at its height, and I felt obligated to defend my dad and all those who were serving. I knew that the truth wasn't as simple as the slogans that protestors were screaming; my father had told me plenty of stories that proved it. He had unofficially adopted an orphanage in Vietnam, and my brothers and sisters and I gathered clothing and sent boxes and boxes of it for him to distribute. And he very much wanted to adopt a little boy that he'd become fond of, until the difficulties of adding one more child to an already full household dissuaded him.

My family and I watched the evening news together, and names like Pleiku, Da Nang, and Quang Tri became part of our regular dinner table conversation. At night I'd have nightmares of a car rolling up to the front door with military personnel bearing the worst news possible; during the day I resented having to be so responsible. But I was the oldest, and it was what I did. We carried on. We were a military family.

One day a car did roll up, and two officers in uniform got out. I thought my heart would stop beating on the spot. My dad was alive but had been evacuated out of the country because of a serious fungal infection. Little did we know at that time that there was much more to the story. My father was responsible for installing and maintaining communication cables throughout the northern third of South Vietnam, and he was in charge of the outposts scattered throughout that territory. He traveled to each one by helicopter, determined to lead from the front. Installation and maintenance of the cables required defoliation of the areas in which they were installed, and Agent Orange was used to do the job. He was awash in it, as were many of the soldiers under his command. Twenty years later, he would be diagnosed with Parkinson's disease, which ultimately resulted in his death in 2006. He is now considered a delayed casualty of the Vietnam War.

After my father returned from Vietnam, he and my mother noticed that the stress of constant relocation had started to manifest in some of my siblings, so they decided to seek more stability for our family. My father was accepted into a doctoral program at Arizona State University, and we made the transition to Mesa, Arizona. This would be the last family move.

Together, my parents and their indomitable warrior spirits set the standard for how we lived our lives, and how their grandchildren were to live theirs. Two of their children, myself included, went on to serve. Of twenty grandchildren, seven are in active military service. Three of us married members of the military. And so the legacy continues. My siblings and I and our children couldn't forget the credo that my mother and father lived by if we tried.

Do your duty. Love your country. Live with honor. Suck it up.

As much as I had screamed that I hated military life when we were back in Germany in the sixties, my parents' legacy ultimately motivated me to serve, and I chose to apply for an Air Force ROTC scholarship in 1976 as I pursued an MBA. I found myself in field training in the summer of 1977, the first year ROTC was coed. It was during that training summer in Kansas that I had one of those accidental but meant-to-be life-defining moments. Women were just beginning pilot training that summer, and there was a lot of angst about women in the cockpit. I was scheduled to fly in the T-37 jet trainer. As luck would have it, smoke filled the interior of my plane as I taxied out with my instructor. I now had the privilege of completing my first emergency evacuation.

The powers-that-be scurried to procure another aircraft, and the new instructor just happened to know a pilot who lived in my hometown. The pilot who lived in my hometown just happened to fly sailplanes. When I heard his name, I laughed out loud; my neighbors had been trying to get me to go on a blind date with the guy for two years. The next time I was home, I called him, he took me up in a sailplane, and thirty-seven years later Courtney Brye and I continue navigating our life together.

Just like I knew that I would never become a mother, I knew that I would ultimately marry a stay-at-home kind of a guy, someone with roots who would not require me to pack my bags every year and gallop around the country. That's exactly what I thought I got when I married that dashing former Air Force pilot, who had decided that it was time to settle down and raise a family on a farm even as he continued to fly for a commercial airline. And that's how we eventually found ourselves in bucolic farm country on the northwestern edge of the Appalachians. Never mind that I knew nothing about raising pigs, chicken, or cattle. I got on-the-job training in all sorts of useful skills, from dealing with snakes in the hen house to separating two fighting bulls. (Lesson learned in that case? You don't even try. You grab the kids and go shopping.) I was certain the animals had a sixth sense that told them when Courtney would be away and that they planned their misbehavior accordingly.

I loved the predictable rhythms of our life on the farm, but at the same time, I felt a little restless. We took as many trips with our kids as we could, traveling to national parks in order to hike and camp and climb mountains, and to battleground sites and Washington, DC, to learn about history. In the nation's capital, we visited the Vietnam Memorial, where Courtney's best friend's name was inscribed on The Wall. Attending the National Memorial Day Concert on the West Lawn of the US Capitol became a family tradition.

Life continued in a busy whirlwind of activities—sports, school, adventures, and farm chores. Through it all, Courtney and I tried to be dreamkeepers, focusing on supporting our children's passions rather than admonishing them to be "realistic." Early on it became clear that we had at least one child who was following in his father's military aviator footsteps. We were happy for Eric when he received his appointment to the Naval Academy, and so very proud of him.

And then along came 9/11. By the end of that horrible day, the world was a different place. On a personal level, my son's role in the military had changed from peacetime soldier to future active-duty combatant, and the ripple effect of the violent attacks would alter my entire family's life in profound and unimaginable ways. Not only did those ripples lead my other children into military service, but ultimately, they also led both my husband and me to live in a war zone.

In July of 2010, I moved to Afghanistan to teach science and related courses in an English-speaking school in Kabul. The previous year I had visited Courtney in Afghanistan, where he was living and working for Safi Airways. On that first visit to Kabul in 2009, I had been moved and touched by the people I met there, finding them every bit as hospitable and generous as Courtney had told me they were. After I returned home from that trip, I prepared for another year of teaching science in my local school district. From the outside things looked the same, but really they were different. *I* was different. I couldn't get Afghanistan out of my mind.

The school year began, and I stayed busy teaching, advising parents on the USNA-Parents listserv, and keeping track of my kids. Courtney was still in Kabul, but at least now I could picture where he was and I knew the people who were working side by side with him. And then one day I came to a realization: I was lonely in my empty nest. I did not want to spend another year alone.

Courtney had been away for almost two years, and that was enough. Eric and Jordan, our two oldest sons, were on active duty.

Katrina, our next child, had cross-commissioned into the Air Force, and Brendan, our youngest, was still in college training as a helicopter pilot. Our nephew was now attending school in Arizona, and so our house, once so full of life, laughter, and dirty clothes, echoed in its emptiness. Neither my nephew nor my kids were likely to make it home for any meaningful length of time, so there was nothing to tie me to the farm other than the farm itself.

Courtney was convinced that the efforts to build a transportation infrastructure in Afghanistan were starting to make a difference in its fragile economy. As far as improving the lives of its people in any kind of permanent way, education had to be part of the answer. I was a teacher, I reasoned, so maybe I could contribute in my own small way to a positive change.

So I moved to Afghanistan in July of 2010 to spend more time with Courtney and to respond to a calling I'd felt when I visited him there the previous year. But I had another reason, too, and it was just as important. One of my children had already served there, and it didn't seem like much of a stretch to think that others might follow. I wanted to better understand that country, so monumentally different from our own. *Knowledge is power,* I told myself. I would not be deployed, but I would be *there,* sandals on the ground, and I might learn some things that would help me cope with my children's deployments there, and help me help them, too. A military mom is always on duty.

It's been almost fourteen years since my oldest child set foot on the grounds of the US Naval Academy as a new member of the military. In the past nearly decade and a half, I have learned a thing or two about being a military mom. I have counseled my children and the children of others through discouragement, disappointment, and grief, and I've celebrated sweet victories with them. I've endured their multiple deployments—eight as of this writing, a possible ninth coming up, and who knows how many more in the future.

With so many deployments and trainings behind me, I've learned how to say goodbye. My children know that my goodbye is more than just a farewell. It's a command; it's a blessing; it's a prayer. "Be safe," I say, and they know that I mean *Don't do anything without thinking* and *Make sure you use your training.* They know I mean *Be careful, I love you,* and *Don't be a cowboy.* And when I write "Be Safe, Love Mom," as I do at the end of every e-mail, every letter, and every note that goes into a care package, I like to think they can hear my voice and feel my arms around them.

I imagine that your heart whispers *Be Safe,* too.

I am intimately familiar with the complex tangle of emotions that we mothers experience starting the moment our children announce their intention to serve in the US military: pride, fear, hope, anxiety, worry, surprise, frustration, and love to name a few; I'm sure you can add some of your own. And maybe you, dear reader, are feeling one or two—or three or four—of these emotions as you read this. Maybe you would like a companion sitting next to you on this roller-coaster ride for which your child has volunteered you. Whether you have one child in uniform or, like me, multiple children in a variety of uniforms, I'm guessing you could use some words of guidance and encouragement. I'm guessing you could use some hard-to-come-by information laced with the occasional bit of humor. I'll do my best in the pages that follow to translate my lifetime of having loved ones in the military into useful bits of advice. I'll share stories from other mothers on this same adventure, and suggest some practical steps you can take to make your life easier. I'll tell you the truth, because that is what you need and deserve. And one of the first truths that I want you to know is that you are not in this alone.

So come, sit. Let's join forces and talk. There are some things I want to share with you.

Letting Go

You're in the Army, Navy, Air Force, Marines Now

*I*t's Induction Day—I-Day—at the US Naval Academy, and twelve hundred freshmen, or plebes, swarm the storied campus in Annapolis, the sum of them as anxious and bumbling as a group of directionless hornets. These young men and women, most fresh out of high school, are accompanied by clusters of loved ones—parents, grandparents, siblings, girlfriends, and boyfriends—who hover around them, glancing at watches and counting down the moments until the appointed hour. The hour when they will have to say goodbye.

After a year of intense applications, examinations, nominations, and—finally!—acceptance into the US Naval Academy, the new students are embarking on Plebe Summer, a six-week training program that will prepare them for the grueling four-year regimen of academics and military training that follows.

When my oldest son, Eric, and I rose at 5:30 that morning, the July air was already warm and sticky. It had been a late night. In one final mom-in-charge act, I'd insisted that Eric have all of his high school graduation thank-you cards sent before he left for the Academy, and by the time the final envelopes were sealed and the last of the stamps were licked it was two A.M. Yet our collective excited (Eric's) and anxious (mine) energy propelled us out of bed a few hours later and off we went to join the other plebes and parents on the Yard, as the grounds of the Naval Academy are called. I'd made a fifty-dollar bet with Eric, ever the stoic—a quality that would serve him well during Plebe Summer and beyond—that I wouldn't cry that day. And I did make it dry-eyed through our final words and last hug, and even as he strode toward the doors of the in-processing building, I held it together. But as soon as he disappeared through those doors, the tears flowed.

I cried for myself and the end of an era as I watched my oldest son embark on his first major life adventure without me. And I cried for Eric, tears of raw pride. He'd worked so hard to get here—not just over the last year or so during the tedious and nerve-wracking application process, but for the past eighteen years, when every decision, life lesson, and effort he'd made seemed to be delivering him to this very moment. It was a day nearly two decades in the making.

I didn't have much time to indulge my tears, though—I had a plebe to stalk. I-Day is as much an induction for the parents as it is for the plebes, and families are given a glimpse of the summer in store for the inductees through demonstrations and programs throughout the day. All the while, we parents "follow" the plebes around campus, hoping to catch sight of our sons and daughters as they go through the induction rituals.

So I struggled to pull myself together, a task made more difficult by the fact that my very calm and collected husband, the yin to my yang, was halfway around the world dropping our thirteen-year-old daughter Katrina off for a summer exchange program in Norway.

Eric, meanwhile, received his Alpha number, collected his standard issue uniforms, boots, sneakers, and manuals, and sat in front of the Navy barbers as they quickly and methodically shaved off his hair. All was relatively calm until he met his detailers, or upper class trainers, who immediately and loudly got in his face and required him to address them with sir or ma'am "sandwiches." He "Sir-yes-Sir!"ed and "Ma'am-yes-Ma'am!"ed his way through the instruction on how to salute and the recitation of the mission of the US Naval Academy.

The long hot summer had begun.

I was thrilled to spot Eric as he emerged from the hall. He was at once oh-so-familiar (my son!) and yet unfamiliar, freshly shorn and in the white works uniform that resembled a baggy sailor suit. I watched as he climbed dutifully onto one of the several waiting buses along with his fellow newly shorn and outfitted plebes.

Instantly, a memory bloomed in my mind of another emotional day. Another bus.

Eric had watched the big yellow bus ramble by on the country road outside our farm in rural Ohio each school morning for a few years, and he was growing more impatient every day to be one of the "big kids" who got to ride on that yellow bus. I took perhaps a bit too much pleasure in explaining that he was not a "big kid" yet, and so it wasn't his turn. I was quite content to keep him with me at home; I relished our days of chores mixed with the simple joys of raising kids on a farm, and I wished they would never end.

Not to mention the fact that I was a bit of a momma grizzly bear, slightly distrustful of anything or anyone who could possibly harm my cubs.

From the moment I discovered I was pregnant for the first time, my response to motherhood had been primal, instinctive, raw. During each of my four pregnancies, I took far better care of myself than I ever had before. When my children were infants, I kept them well-fed, clean, and healthy. I read to them, baby-proofed the house, and bought infant car seats before they were required. As they grew and participated in almost every sport known to man, I bought protective gear: face guards, mouth guards, shin guards, chest protectors, and helmets. Courtney and I monitored Internet access and had the children fingerprinted. Fingerprinted? That's right. We were covering all of our bases in case a child ever went missing. Whatever it took to keep our children safe and thriving, I did.

As challenging and exhausting as those early years with four young ones were, they were also wonderful. In part because the kids were curious and funny and they kept me on my toes. But also in part—and I'm leveling with you here—because I was in control. I decided where they would go and with whom they would play. I was the queen of their castle, and I liked it that way.

But then the day came when Eric was one of those "big kids," the day when the big yellow bus would be stopping at our house. That September morning, Courtney and I walked him down our long driveway, his too-big backpack bouncing on his back. His two younger siblings (Brendan was not yet born) were crammed in the red wagon, excited to ride along and witness this thrilling event: the first of the chicks to leave the nest. We took pictures, first of Eric alone beaming at the camera, and then of Eric and me, and then of Eric and Courtney. When the big yellow bus roared to a stop alongside our mailbox and the accordion door wheezed open, I forced a beaming smile as he climbed aboard with all those other kids. The door closed, and we waved and waved, and I could see his little blonde head bobbing in the window as the bus disappeared into the distance.

Then I burst into tears. *How could I keep him safe? What if he got hurt and I wasn't there to rescue him? And what about the mean kids who might tease him or teach him bad words? And what if his teacher didn't understand that he was the sun and the moon and the stars?* As I dissolved into a weepy mess, Courtney began to laugh. "You can't keep him home forever," he said, reaching his arm around me.

Those words would echo in my mind's chambers time and time again over the next few decades.

They echoed when Jordan, our second son—who completed the rigorous application process to the Naval Academy only as a Plan B—was admitted and decided to accept his appointment to the academy. Except this time, things were different. We were a nation at war. Since Eric's induction into the Academy two years prior, our country had endured the September 11th terrorist attacks and we were now in the early days of the War on Terror. The atmosphere in the country—and in the military—was charged, and the stakes of sending a child into the military seemed higher. I was worried—was Jordan feeling pressured to accept the appointment? Was this really the right choice for him? But Courtney's words scrolled through my mind, reminding me of what I already knew. I couldn't keep him home forever. How could I hold him back from doing his duty? And so two years after Eric's and my journey to Annapolis on his I-Day, I said goodbye to my second son—at 6'5", head and shoulders above most of his fellow plebes—on the hallowed grounds of the Yard.

By the time Katrina graduated from high school, I'd already sent two children off to the Naval Academy, so you would think I would be used to the letting-go process. As it turns out, supporting your child's decision to join the military is a lot like childbirth. You remember that it was painful, but the reward was so great you forget just how just how bad the whole process really was. Then, suddenly, after months of preparation, you're in the thick of it and it hurts like *hell* and you wonder why in the world you ever agreed to put yourself through this again.

Brendan, our youngest, assured us through his childhood and teenage years that he was not the least bit interested in the military. He was tired of being the fourth Brye, and tired of everyone asking him—again and again and again—if he planned to attend the Naval Academy, too. There was no way he was going to apply, he responded, much to my great secret relief. I was not sure how much more this heart could take. So you can imagine my shock when I found him at his computer one afternoon applying for the Army ROTC Helicopter Scholarship at the University of North Dakota. The military? The Army? Helicopters? My dad spent part of my childhood flying all over northern South Vietnam in Hueys—or "those damn Hueys," as my mother always referred to them—and I had a good sense of how dangerous helicopters were. It's no exaggeration to say that from the time Courtney and I even started to contemplate marriage and children, I was already thinking, *Please, God, no kids in helos.*

You know the rest of the story. Brendan represents Army in the dinner table battles over which branch of the service is dominant. And he flies the Chinook helo, the biggest in the Army arsenal. Everyone has his or her bragging rights.

Four kids, four dogs in the fight.

*H*ow did a mom who had a hard time letting her kindergartner climb aboard the big yellow school bus end up with four children serving in the military, and serving all over the world, no less? This is a question I get often from military moms, who are hopeful that over the years I've discovered the grand secret—that special phrase, that meditative chant, that daily ritual, the work-around, the shortcut—that makes the act of letting go, the idea of offering your kids up to the US military, easy. But I don't have a grand secret. All I know is this: you just do it. You do it even though it's hard, and overwhelming. You do it even though it's scary. You do it with a shaky smile on your face and a whispered *Be safe* on your lips. You do it even though it breaks your heart.

*E*very spring, as the new batch of Naval Academy plebes and their parents begin to prepare for Plebe Summer, the freshman parents join the listserv, and I am bombarded with questions of all kinds.

What should my son or daughter pack?

See the Permit to Report Guide for the complete list.

Is there anything else he or she should pack?

No. The list is complete.

Should I label his or her clothes?

No, your plebe will take care of it.

What about banking?

Your plebe will take care of it.

What about laundry?

Your plebe will take care of it.

And on and on. I know by now that these questions are thinly veiled prompts for me to address what these parents are really wondering—the questions that are actually keeping them awake at night: *What is my role now? Do I have any control? Will my child be safe? And happy?* The core issues associated with letting go—grief, fear, and anxiety—are so easily buried under piles of To Do lists.

And then weeks later, during the long hot nights of Plebe Summer, I receive more questions from parents on the listserv. This time, they are emotional, confessional. Many parents are distressed and anxious, and they're hoping to find a safe place to confess their feelings. *I miss my daughter so much. I can't get through the day without crying*, one might write. Or *I don't understand what is happening to me. I am normally in control. Why do I feel so overwhelmed?* In the subtleties of these emails are hints of surprise, embarrassment, and sometimes even shame. *Am I crazy?* They seem to say. *Am I alone in feeling this way?*

No, you are not crazy. And you are not alone. I want to shout this from the rooftops.

You're overwhelmed, I write, *because it's overwhelming.* When a child leaves home for college or a job, it can be an unsettling and sad transition, even if it's exciting, too. *Your* child has just left home not just for college, or for a job, but in order to become a warrior, to willingly fight in some of the most dangerous places and situations in the world. It makes sense that the experience feels daunting to you, even harrowing. And of course you miss your son or daughter. Of course you do.

Every military career begins with a grueling, intense, and agonizing initiation period—whether it's Plebe Summer in Annapolis or boot camp on Parris Island. It's designed this way because our sons and daughters must immediately and irreversibly strip themselves of their old identities, their former lives. Because life as they know it will never be the same.

The same is true for the families back home. While our loved ones are away, acclimating to their new lives as soldiers, we also are undergoing our own initiation period, adjusting to our new identities as military mothers and fathers and wives and children. The shock of this new life is not absorbed more easily just because we have the comforts of home and other family and friends around us. The loss is just the same. Letting go—of our sons and daughters, of our control, of our old lives—requires the courage of a warrior and the endurance of a marathoner. We need to understand that we are at the beginning of a long and steep road.

I do know this: after you take the first step on that long and steep road, the second step will follow. And then the third, and the fourth, and eventually, the process will be almost as automatic as breathing: one foot will follow the other, again and again and again. Each day you'll wake up and letting go will get just a tiny bit easier.

But you must take that first step. You must let your children climb aboard that bus to follow their calling. And we will all march on.

Becoming a Warrior

"I almost drowned today, Mom," the phone call begins.

With those words, I, too, am immediately disoriented; I feel the weight of the water pressing hard against my chest, and I can't seem to get enough air.

The voice on the other end of the line belongs to Brendan, who begins to describe his experience that day in the dunk tank—one of the many training obstacles that those who pursue the coveted wings of a military aviator must overcome before they ever get to an aircraft.

To survive a plane crash in water, a military pilot must be able to exit the aircraft no matter how disoriented he or she is, hence the dunk tank—an exercise in which the future pilot is submerged multiple times in a rotating aircraft shell. Then, underwater and in darkness, he or she must find the way out. As would be the case in a real accident, the pilot candidates don't know when they'll go under, so they might not have had time to take in a big lungful of air—which makes it even more urgent to find a way to escape and make it to the top. There are rescue divers ready to assist, but if the candidates don't make it on their own, they can be failed out of flight school. It's a harrowing experience for potential aviators—and their mothers. All of my boys have endured it, which means, by extension, so have I. Three times.

During our phone call that late summer evening, Brendan described how, during one of his multiple twisting submersions, the trainer rotated in an unexpected direction and he gulped water instead of air. He clawed at the seat buckles, fighting to release himself, but his mind and his fingers were having a hard time working. And then, praise be, all of his training kicked in. All of that discipline, memorization, and determination took over, and he found his way to the helo hatch and made it out and up. He could breathe again. And—on the other end of the phone line—so could I.

Life as a military mom all too often resembles dunk tank training. There are days, weeks, and months when life is relatively "normal," but you live each day a bit on edge, knowing that at any moment you could be submerged into the darkness, searching for the surface and trying to find your breath.

I was first plunged into the military mom dunk tank on Eric's Induction Day at the Naval Academy. I thought I had known what to expect. I grew up in the military. My husband had been in the military. *I* had been in the military. But as Eric and his classmates marched through the doors of Bancroft Hall to the solemn beat of a drum at the end of I-Day—oh my. You can think forward and plan and prepare for the moment, but when that reality hits you, you might as well be groping for the helo hatch and trying to find which way is up.

Being a military mom means a whole new way of thinking and a whole new way of feeling, not to mention a whole new acronym-filled language. *What the heck does TDY mean? Or BUD/S, ACU, or DITY?* More importantly: *How do I prepare for those first two weeks of boot camp or basic training or Plebe Summer when no phone contact between the new military member and his or her family is allowed? How can I get used to the idea that my child is being screamed at? How can I ever cope with the idea that his or her ultimate destination could be on a battlefield? How can I bear the thought that my baby, the child I nurtured and protected from birth, might never come back home?*

Isolation. Darkness. Disorientation. *Which way is up?*

At the Naval Academy, Plebe Summer is six weeks, and it's six weeks of indoctrination into a world of exhaustion, meaningless tasks, memorization, recitation, physical endurance training, infrequent communication with loved ones, and never, ever doing anything right the first (or maybe even the tenth) time. Plebes learn to operate under stress, to follow orders, and to operate as a team. They learn military etiquette and attention to detail. The same skills, values, and rules are taught at boot camp or basic training of any kind.

The truth is that just as our sons and daughters endure their rigorous basic training rituals in order to become warriors, we moms are also warriors-in-training, enlisted in our own Military Mom Basic Training program. We need to develop our muscles, gird our loins, and become battle-hardened, just like our kids. And we can do it, but it takes work and a whole lot of grit.

Lynn, the mother of a Marine, thought she knew what I-Day meant. Having a dad who was retired Army, a brother who was a Marine, and another brother in the Air Force, she understood that I-Day meant her daily parenting job was over. Still, she attempted to mentally prepare for months before the big day. She googled everything she could about the Naval Academy and tried to brace herself for the moment her son would hug her goodbye. "I am slightly vain," Lynn said, "and even though tons of other moms said do *not* wear makeup on Induction Day, I thought I knew better. So we walk up to the BIG sign that says *No Parents Beyond This Point*. I wasn't crying until my son turned to me and gave me a hug, and then I completely lost it. The tears came so hard and fast that people were staring at me. For a second I thought to scream, 'Hey, that's my kid. Give him back!' but as the idea flitted through my brain, someone pointed a news camera at me and someone else shoved a microphone in my face and asked me how I was feeling. Apparently, every year the press preys on that over-the-top train wreck parent at the point of goodbye. Well, that year, sobbing and with black eye makeup smeared all over my face, I won the Train Wreck Mom award.

"Then the news truck left and this beautiful man in a crisp white uniform walked over to me and attempted to calm my nerves. He told me they'd take great care of my son. Who was this man who said he could take care of my baby? Yep, it was only the Commandant of Midshipmen, the man in charge of all 4,500 Naval Academy mids. As I slowly composed myself, I looked around and realized that my son had made it to his dream. And since I wanted for him what he wanted for himself, that meant that I had made it to mine, too."

Many of us are thunderstruck when our kids tell us that they want to enter the military. Even if you are from a military family, it can still be a shock, although at least you're on somewhat familiar territory. You know the rules. The overriding rule, the one everyone needs to know first, is:

There are rules for everything.

Subsidiary Rules:
1) *Don't walk on the grass. That's what sidewalks are for.*
2) *The more stripes, stars, and stuff on their covers (hats), the more important they are.*
3) *The military will issue you everything you need. Mothers are not an issued item.*

If you are not from a military family, this new world can feel like a brand new planet. And your child's decision to become a resident of this planet can be even more puzzling. The experience of June, another Marine Corps mom, was especially daunting. "I am sure there are many moms that come from a long history of family members serving in their nation's military. I was not such a mom. Because of circumstances, my parents and grandparents were never in the armed forces. In fact, they were in internment camps in the middle of the Mojave Desert during World War II. I didn't have family experience to draw from. I was constantly asked, 'Why are you allowing your son to join the Marines?' People couldn't comprehend that I wasn't 'allowing' him to join the military; I was 'allowing' him to follow his dreams. There is a major difference between the two."

I wonder how, given her family background, June ever had the strength and compassion to arrive at this distinction. What an act of motherly love. What a warrior mother.

During Military Mom Basic Training, we learn to let go—or at least to try to let go, to *start* to let go. Our sudden lack of control over our son's or daughter's safety and destiny becomes painfully obvious, as we have no access to our kids at all for the first two weeks of their training, and no communication for the entire six weeks except three brief phone calls at scheduled times, and a few—very few—letters. I did receive one letter from Eric during his Plebe Summer, a letter he was required to write: *Hi Mom. I am alive. I am fine. Very respectfully Midn 4/c Eric Brye.*

This loss of communication can be traumatic. We have no way of knowing how they're doing, what they're feeling, and whether or not they're succeeding. We have no idea if they're contemplating quitting. In other words, *woosh*, into the dunk tank we go.

Isolation. Darkness. Disorientation. *Which way is up?*

Melinda, a Navy mom, shared that when her daughter started boot camp, the pain and anxiety she felt were relentless. "I felt like my heart had been ripped out of my body. There was no way to communicate except for a few brief phone calls and letters, and it was the first time in my life as a mom was I not able to stay in touch with my daughter. The only time I had rest from my anxiety was the two days I spent doing colonoscopy prep." Colonoscopy prep? Sign me up. It sounds so much better than the massive letting go we have to do when we surrender our kids to the military. And when my kids are deployed, sometimes I think it might be easier to just crawl into bed, go to sleep, and wake up when it's all over.

The trauma of such severe disconnection from our children comes in tsunami-sized waves. The question is: What do you do with those feelings? How do you cope, reach out, grab onto a lifeline? The first part of your training in becoming a warrior mother is to learn to trust in the process. The military has been training warriors for a long time, and you need to trust, as hard as it may be, that there is a purpose behind all of the rules, regulations, and hardships.

So let's look at some of those hard-to-understand, hard-to-accept practices.

What's all the screaming about? Being able to operate in a stress-filled environment rationally, without getting flustered or emotional, is an essential skill for a warrior. If you can function effectively when someone is literally screaming in your face, you're building the muscles you need to do just that. No matter what happens, warriors need to think logically—to find the seat belt buckles even though they can't breathe. I understand that thinking rationally is not always easy for the mothers of warriors, especially when our primal protective instincts kick in. But we need to learn that skill as much as our children do.

Why do they need to make their beds, or change their uniforms, twenty times a day? Because they need to do it until they do it right. "Almost" isn't good enough. Attention to detail is critical. A crease in the blanket or a piece of lint on the uniform is simply not acceptable. Why not? Because when performing a preflight checklist, skipping a step or ignoring a piece of debris on the runway can be life threatening. Not cleaning a weapon properly can have disastrous consequences. In a world filled with "almost is good enough," our warriors must learn to perform at 100 percent. And we must understand this and not discourage it or complain about it.

What about physical performance? Why are they pushed so hard? Warriors must know beyond the shadow of a doubt that they can push themselves way out of their comfort zones. Life on the front lines is not easy. The enemy is not going to lighten up just so that our troops will be comfortable. Our loved ones will be too hot or too cold, and they'll be hungry, dirty, and stressed. Staying hunkered down in a foxhole for hours on end is physically taxing. So is wearing fifty pounds of body armor in 110-degree heat. Standing watch all night in the cold is uncomfortable. So is living in a tent with no hot meals for weeks on end. Our troops need to be able to stay focused in spite of their discomfort in order to do their jobs, and there's nothing like experience to help them prepare. Being uncomfortable is a good thing when it builds your endurance for the future. Our warriors need to know that they have it in themselves to stick it out.

Why is such a big deal made over the Honor Code? A soldier or sailor or aviator must tell the truth. Always. Lying could put one's shipmates or company mates or wingmen at risk. Out of adherence to the Honor Code comes trust. You have to be able to trust the sentry on watch. You have to be able to trust your wingman. You have to be able to trust your shipmates. Without trust, a unit cannot function.

The list of questions and concerns about training practices goes on and on. And even though they may not make sense to us from the outside, you have to learn to trust that these hard-to-fathom practices and rules are pushing our children to become extraordinary.

We want our children to be extraordinary. We want them to be their best. It's why we carpooled to all those faraway travel soccer games, and helped with homework, and served as room mothers and PTA moms and all those other things. So now—even though it's a scary thought and it means fighting the urge to protect them—*we need it to be hard.* No short cuts! We want them pushed to their limits when they're in a protected harbor—boot camp or ROTC or basic training or a service academy—and not out on a battlefield not knowing what they are capable of. The difficulties they encounter in a protected harbor might just save their lives and the lives of their buddies.

My boys are aviators. That means they each had to attend a three-week survival training known as SERE, which stands for survival, evasion, resistance, and escape. What happens is secret, but Courtney had also endured the training, so I had a vague idea of what to expect. The participants would learn survival techniques, try to evade, get captured, and try to escape. They would be tortured and try to resist. The decision to become an aviator suddenly takes on a whole new meaning when you start to consider—and experience— what might actually happen if you're shot down.

Those trainings were the longest three weeks of not only my sons' lives but of mine. Each time one of my boys began the ordeal I felt like I was swimming deep underwater without an oxygen tank. It was sort of like being in a dunk tank for three weeks: no way to breathe, no way to withstand the pressure, no way to get to the surface. I tried to cram my schedule so full that I had no time to think about what they were enduring. That notion was ridiculous, of course; there's always time to worry about your children, whether it's in the middle of a sleepless night, or when your attention drifts from the conversation or task at hand, or in your nightmares. Eric was in the desert—snakes, heat exhaustion, no food sources. Jordan was in Maine in January—thirty degrees below zero and three feet of snow. Brendan was in the Alabama swamp—gators, more snakes, putrefaction.

Each time a son emerged from the training and called me, the relief was overpowering. I cried, I laughed, I felt the tension pour out of my body. All three of them lost more than twenty pounds, but all three of them made it through. I don't remember exactly what they said when they called; all I know is that I was overwhelmed with emotion. Not only had they survived, but I had, too. I'd made it to the surface, and I could breathe again.

How did my sons endure those unbearable three weeks? They learned to "embrace the suck," which is advice we warrior moms need to heed as well. It's best if we learn how to cope with difficult things as early in our children's enlistments as possible, because bigger things are coming in the future. Like when you might go months on end without hearing from your child, and when you are not even allowed to know where he or she is. Like when a missed call designation on your phone will bring you to tears. Like when the nightmares that wake you in the middle of the night threaten to overwhelm you. Like when you go to the funeral of the child of another mother.

We want it to be hard immediately, without delay, so that they are ready when they need to be, and so that we are, too.

So how, exactly, when I feel like I'm drowning in worries about my children and their safety, do I simultaneously "embrace the suck" and free myself from the darkness of the military mom dunk tank? I find it incredibly useful in those challenging times to remember the characters of the kids I raised and all of the adversities and hardships they've overcome to deliver them to this moment, whatever "this moment" may be, whether it's a form of basic training, advanced training, a deployment, or some other challenge. Often, I think of their lives growing up on our farm.

Farm life provides a great foundation for future military officers. The endless and repetitive chores teach the importance of endurance, persistence, humility, and cooperation. Stacking bales in the top of the mow prepares a young man or woman for the dusts of Afghanistan. Racing a thunderstorm to get the last wagon in before the storm hits is pretty similar to the stress of a carrier landing. And feeding the animals before you feed yourself is good preparation for automatically taking care of the men and women in your command. If you can catch a calf, you can do an obstacle course. And if you shoot groundhogs, that experience might help when you travel with a weapon in your thigh holster. When I'm awake in the middle of the night, I think of all the warrior "training" my kids completed before they ever joined the military, and I can breathe a little easier.

Chances are your children didn't grow up on a farm, but over the years you've undoubtedly watched them develop the skills and qualities that they'll need for lives in uniform, whether or not you realized it at the time. You saw those qualities when your son stood up to the bullies in elementary school and you realized you had raised a champion with a sense of integrity. You saw them when your daughter refused to go along with the mean girls in middle school and treated everyone with fairness and respect instead. You saw them when your high schooler never missed a sports practice, in spite of spending more time on the bench than on the field. You were itching to go up to that coach and give him a piece of your mind, but you knew your kid needed to handle it independently. And he or she did. Your kids have had plenty of lessons in becoming warriors well before I-Day or boot camp, and so have you.

And so I encourage you, when you find yourself suddenly thrust into the dark waters of your own dunk tank, to think of the warrior qualities your child possesses. He or she is strong. Persistent. Committed. Courageous. You know this is not the first time your son or daughter has been tested and tried. And it's not the first time you have, either.

There may be days when you feel you've been plunged into water that's too deep, too rough, too uncertain. Believe me when I say that you have everything you need to navigate these waters. You will grapple with all the uncertainty and the worry. Remember who your children are. Take strength from their strength, and then send back encouragement in return. You will make your way to the surface, to the light, to the safety of the shore.

Semper Gumby

can hear the shouts and screams coming from the midway, the heart of the county fair, where the rides and the carnival games are set up. The Ferris wheel is spinning slowly, giving riders a bird's eye view of the coliseum below. Round one of the demolition derby has just finished there, and the emergency sirens and black smoke rising signify that it must have been a success. What's a demolition derby, after all, without some crushed metal and a fire or two? The music of the carousel beckons, and little ones in strollers wait to climb astride a pink pony or golden unicorn, caramel apples and funnel cakes clutched in sticky fingers. Nearby, an Elvis impersonator has drawn a small crowd.

I am in the rickety wooden building that houses the show arena, where all manner of critters are displayed, promenaded, and judged. As I sit on the splintered bleachers, I remember all of the times I waited for my children to begin the battle of kid versus pig or steer or chicken. There were a lot of those contests, because every August while our kids were young, we spent a week at the fair. We didn't just visit, we camped there, rain or shine, in the heat and the mud and the dust, because our kids showed their animals and had

43

to be on hand to care for them. The higher the animals placed, the more money they would command when they were sold at the end of the week. That money would go straight into their young owners' pockets, so there was a lot at stake. Getting a higher placement required not only becoming proficient in the care of the animal, but also working with it adeptly in the ring. Imagine a 60-pound eight-year-old herding a 220-pound pig in a pen with twenty-five other recalcitrant swine and their young owners. The grit needed to move a large, temperamental hog into the proper place, with several hundred people watching in the stands—all the while keeping an eye on the judge—cannot be overstated. It was always extremely hot and dirty, and you never knew if the animal, whatever it was, would just lose it and go crazy. The memory of eleven-year-old Katrina being dragged across the pen by her steer, who suddenly went nuts in the ring one August afternoon (she hated him and he knew it), still makes me hyperventilate. A 4-H volunteer jumped over the fence and was allowed to hold the halter while Katrina stuck by that angry beast, tears streaming into her pigtails.

The memory almost brings *me* to tears, too, at least for a moment. But then I blink and remember that my daughter is sitting right next to me with her own baby on her lap. And most of "the brothers," as she calls them, are here, too. In fact, everyone who could get leave is within a stone's throw. We adults roam the barns while the grandkids pet the sheep and learn to jump over steaming piles of cow manure. For three days, we eat the kind of wonderfully unhealthy food you never eat at any other time of the year—fried ice cream, real old-fashioned fair fries, elephant ears, and cotton candy. It's just like Christmas!

Actually, for us, it *is* Christmas. Between the steer show on Wednesday and the combine derby on Sunday, we set aside a day to recreate a Christmas morning gift extravaganza, exchanging the under-$10 gifts we've collected all year long. Early that morning, I bake our family's traditional Christmas cinnamon rolls, and we munch on them all day long. At some point we take a family picture with everyone crammed on the hall stairs in their pajamas, although it's getting harder and harder for all of those six-foot-plus bodies to fit, and now there are more and more little ones filling in the gaps. Rowdy, boisterous tickling and shoving and laughter fill up the house once again, even if it's just for brief moment.

Christmas in August? Who ever heard of such a thing? Well, for me in my crazy, we-need-to-find-a-way-to-get-the-family-together, bend-without-breaking life, Christmas at the county fair in August makes perfect sense. In celebrating special occasions whenever we can find a moment to get most of the family together, I am heeding the unofficial motto of all military parents, a motto that will make your life easier as soon as you learn to embrace it fully: *Semper Gumby*. Always flexible. And just like the lovable little green Gumby doll who can bend and flex in unbelievable ways, we military moms learn to stand on our heads with our legs twisted around our necks to do what we can to preserve the strength of our family ties.

Almost all parents who relinquish their precious son or daughter to military service experience some degree of difficulty when it comes to letting go of planning, of neat orderly lives, of *control*. Some, like my husband, are fairly relaxed about the transition. Others, serious Type As like you-know-who, ride a roller coaster of emotions and eventually come to understand that they must make a choice. One can choose to be a parent who desperately tries to maintain some semblance (that's all it will be) of control, or one can learn to embrace Semper Gumby.

Although I've done a lot of work to transition to the Semper Gumby lifestyle, I sometimes slip back into my "need to know/ need to plan" nature and attempt to schedule forward. You name it: vacations, travel, and family celebrations of all kinds. But I've learned—sometimes (most of the time) the hard way—that much of my planning is futile. Unexpected deployments happen. Changes in training schedules disrupt the best laid plans. I have to let go, or it will drive me crazy. I can't control what is happening to my military son or daughter. I can only control my response to the last-minute changes, the unknowns, and the challenges that lie ahead.

Holidays are often the first occasions that require us to be Gumbyesque. Our kids may be absent because they're deployed or because their presence is required at their duty station. Fortunately, every year when the holidays roll around I can hear my mom's voice saying to me, exactly as she did when I was a little girl and my father was deployed during Christmas again, "It's just a day on the calendar, Elaine. Don't make too much of it." And I say to myself, "That's right, it *is* just a day on the calendar."

In true Semper Gumby spirit, we moms twist and turn and do all kinds of things to make holidays happen, whether or not they happen when the calendar says they do. Like the Navy mom friend of mine who had her Christmas tree up until her son got home from deployment. "He was due home in January, so it sounded like a good idea at the time. But there were deployment extensions after extensions, and by the time he arrived in May that tree was still up. There were no needles left and we no longer plugged in the lights, but we had a tree, by golly!"

Another of my friends has found an unusually creative way of keeping her son with the family during holidays. She has what is essentially a giant poster of her son's head attached to the end of a stick. The family first used it at the son's West Point graduation as a way to find each other in the crowds. But now, at every holiday or family event, they take pictures of him (well, the cardboard him) there with the rest of the family. "It may sound a little silly, but that acknowledgment that he is here with us helps take away some of the sting. And when he sees the pictures, he knows we're thinking of him."

A huge part of Semper Gumby is letting go of the expectation that family milestone events mean that everyone will be there together. I find this a particularly bitter pill to swallow. The year that Jordan was a plebe at the Naval Academy and Eric, two years ahead of him, was a detailer (one of the upperclassman who is responsible for training the incoming class of plebes) was the year that my parents celebrated their fiftieth wedding anniversary. Being an "experienced" military mother by that time (famous last words, but that's how I felt), I had planned our big celebration around the Naval Academy calendar. And then the academy changed its schedule, adding an event that required all plebes to be on campus over the weekend of our family event. I was not happy. Let me rephrase that, I was *ticked*. This was a once-in-a-lifetime celebration that I had planned specifically around the boys' availability, and now the Navy changes its mind? *Grrrr.*

So I did what any Type A mom would do. I tried to find a way around it. I understood (sort of) why Jordan, the plebe, could not attend, but surely Eric, the detailer, could get leave. He quickly shut the idea down. "I can't leave my plebes, Mom." And that was that. They missed the anniversary celebration. As it happened, the extended family would not be together again until my father's funeral three years later.

*I*t's a strange situation we moms are in. We have to develop our calluses and get hardened to the hurt but at the same time stay flexible and make the best of what we do have. We have to stretch beyond where we thought we could stretch yet keep our feet firmly planted on the ground. As my own calluses have developed, I've come to accept the reality that if two kids are together with Courtney and me on any given occasion, it's a bonus; three kids together are a bonanza; and four together all at once? Well, that's like winning the lottery. And when I get the message *sorry mom schedule changed I have duty,* I just keep reminding myself to go with the flow. It takes less effort to swim with the current than against it.

So how do we practice Semper Gumby? How do we swim with the current, not against it? First, we learn not to live by a schedule. Actually, that's not entirely true; we learn that life revolves around *their* schedules, not ours. And we don't make set vacation plans; if our kids can get leave, we take time off—if we're able—once we know that the leave is actually happening.

"Ryan found out he had an unexpected port call eight hours away," a Navy mom named Tina once told me, meaning that her son's ship would dock for a few hours in the port. "We dropped everything and drove to meet him for a six-hour visit. I cannot tell you what it was like to see him come down off that ship. I don't know when I will see him again. Those six hours were priceless."

We make ourselves available at all times for possible contact from our sons and daughters. The weird tone that signals an incoming Skype call means *all hands on deck,* and even if it's three A.M. and our hair is sticking up and we stub our toes getting out of bed, nothing is going to get in the way of our answering that call. We keep our cell phones on at all times, and we suspend our ideas of proper etiquette and good manners when it comes to answering them. If a call from our child comes in during the middle of church, well, we answer it. Or if that cell phone rings in a dark, quiet movie theater on Christmas night? Well, we answer that too, like my friend Nancy, a fellow Naval Academy mom, did when her son was deployed in Iraq and she had to practically climb over the people in her row to get to the aisle so she could race outside to hear her son's voice.

At the Naval Academy, the summer after plebe year is the first time the new midshipmen participate in summer training out in the fleet. They are scheduled for two three-week blocks of training, which could take place on a ship or a sub or a sailboat. The midshipmen get a very nicely organized packet of orders with report dates and locations, and worked into the schedule is a thrilling three-week block of time off. Their parents make plans and schedule flights. We parents who have been through this a time or two suggest refundable tickets.

Because at some point, all hell breaks loose. Report dates change. Ships reposition. Plebes report to Japan instead of Florida. They are required to be in Australia in July instead of San Diego in August. Each year, my e-mail inbox fills up with the cries of frustrated parents. And I can only smile sweetly and say "Semper Gumby" and hope they learn the lesson of flexibility soon. Because these changes, as upsetting as they are, are nothing compared to changes in deployment schedules, where it is not a question of which three weeks they might be gone but which nine months they might be gone. One year I was shell-shocked to find out that after a mere five months at home after two six-month deployments in eighteen months, Eric was deploying yet again. We hadn't been expecting another deployment for a full year. And this time it was to an undisclosed location, which I *hate*. I stomped around the living room for a while, whining and complaining. Finally, I was able to remember that bit of wisdom that I so often offer to others: *The decision has been made and you have no control over it. All you can do is control your response to it.* Heeding my own advice actually helped a bit.

Fortunately, as you practice the stretching, the reaching, and the adapting required by life with a child in the military, you do get better at adjusting to the seemingly constant change. And it's critical that we keep practicing, keep flexing, because over time, we military moms realize that scheduling and logistical inconveniences are innocuous compared to some of the more life-changing hands the military can deal you. You never know how the deck will be shuffled and dealt—and what wild cards might be thrown your way.

June is a mentor to me as a military mom. Her son is a Marine aviator. It was his dream to fly attack helicopters, and he studied hard and graduated at the top of his class during basic aviation training. His standing should have warranted the helicopter billet, with scores so high that they would have enabled him to fly jets had he been so inclined. As it turned out, he was assigned to fly C-130s, those monster cargo planes.

"Lesson Number One," June says. "Never assume that your child's wishes will count more than what are known as 'the operational needs of the military.'"

"Lesson Number Two," she continues. "Decisions made for you by the military may turn out to be blessings in disguise if you approach them with an open mind. This has proved true for our family. In other words, always be flexible."

June's experience reminds me of the old Yiddish proverb: "We plan, God laughs." Except in June's, my, and your case, the proverb could translate into "Moms plan, the US military laughs." No matter your preconceived notion about how things will and *should* go—holiday and birthday celebrations, deployment dates and locations, assignment of service community—the military has its own plan for your son or daughter.

And then there's the sobering reality that not all life-changing hands and hugely surprising wild cards that come your way will have been dealt by the military. In 2001, Eric was inducted into the Naval Academy in a time of peace. Less than three months later, 9/11 ushered in a whole new world. As the day unfolded and Americans tried to understand what had happened and what it might mean, I found it harder and harder to suppress my fear. Nobody yet knew how widespread this attack was or would become. If the Pentagon had been targeted, what did that mean for other high-profile military institutions? Most specifically, *what about the Naval Academy?*

In those days plebes were not allowed to have cell phones, and in any event cellular networks were overloaded. I knew from my military upbringing that calling the Naval Academy directly was not appropriate. I was only one of thousands of parents wondering what was happening, and those lines needed to stay open for urgent matters. Finally I called Eric's sponsor dad in Annapolis. (Sponsor parents are assigned to every plebe in order to provide a sort of home away from home that first year, and to help out in various other ways.) Randy, Eric's sponsor dad, was understanding when I asked if he could hear sirens or see smoke. "All is well on the Severn [River]," he told me kindly.

Later, USNA leadership directed all midshipmen to contact home, and upper classmen willingly shared their phones so plebes could call their worried families. I was overjoyed to hear Eric's voice and have confirmation that he was safe, and grateful for the chance to reassure him that both his dad and his uncle, a pilot for American

Airlines, were safe, too. Many at the academy were not so lucky; they had family members who were directly affected by the tragedy. Perhaps the most telling indicator that life on the Yard had changed for good was an instant message my son sent me later that evening: "We are standing watch at every doorway with bayonets, and we don't even know how to use them yet."

It was a new normal, and it was something nobody could have predicted. Those Firsties—Naval Academy seniors in the Class of 2002—who had just been celebrating Parents' Weekend and the start of their last year on the Yard now were heading into war. Their parents were reeling with shock. "All of a sudden my thoughts about my daughter went from pride and pleasure that she was graduating from a fantastic school with an opportunity to serve, to terror because she was headed into combat. It all became real in an instant," one mother told me. Another mom simply said, "We have been looking forward to commissioning for four years, but now I am afraid."

Thus we moms learn to flex, to stretch, and to cope with our fears. We stand on our heads and extend our arms far enough to wrap around our children no matter where they are. We learn to live in the moment, reduce expectations, take joy in the little things, and relish the things that count. We accommodate in ways both big and small.

The reality is that life as a military parent is a lot like being on a roller coaster at the county fair. You can lean forward and scream as you're whipped back and forth and side to side around the twists and turns, but the sooner you sit back and sink into the seat—hands firmly clasped on the protective bar—the better. I know I would prefer it if my kids were all buckled in beside me, but we've moved well beyond that stage. If my children weren't in the military, it would have taken me a little (or a lot) longer to figure out that I can't control the twists and the turns, but I'm sure I would have gotten to that realization eventually.

And so as I celebrate Christmas in the heat of August, the perfume of livestock rather than pine needles lingering in the air, I take a second to acknowledge some of the gifts that the military has given me. It has helped to develop my children into highly qualified leaders. It has given me reasons to be oh-so-proud of their tremendous accomplishments and of the fact that they are serving their country so selflessly. And it has gently supported me (ahem) in becoming a much more flexible person. (I'm only partly joking here.)

Semper Gumby.

From Ballet Slippers
to Combat Boots

She needs to make sure that the hair is just right, that every curl is locked into place and the bun is positioned perfectly on her head. Fortunately, years of recitals have given her lots of practice in getting performance-ready.

I close my eyes and expect to hear the warm-up begin: "First position. *And*. Plié, relevé. Plié, relevé." Instead, a loud voice calling "Attention on deck!" fills the air, and Training Sergeant Katrina Brye, every hair perfectly in place, arrives on the scene in her crisply pressed khaki uniform and proceeds to issue commands. "Drop and give me ten. *Up! Down! Up! Down!*" she shouts as dozens of plebes fall onto their hands and feet and pump out a quick set of push-ups.

Where has this stony-faced, impeccably professional military leader come from? What has caused the transformation from princess into Amazon warrior?

A lot of mothers of military women are profoundly shocked when their daughters—those giggling girls who had Little Mermaid-themed birthday parties and gave tea parties for their dolls—choose a life of weapons and testosterone-charged environments that just might include war. Even if we moms ourselves have served, it's different when it's our little ballerina. But despite the shock, we are in awe as we watch them fight physical limitations, stereotypes, and flat-out discrimination in order to take their places and serve their country. Because after all, we taught them that girls can do anything, from cartwheels on the balance beam to flying an airplane. And if they want that airplane to be an F/A-18 jet instead of a B-757, well then, full speed ahead.

It hasn't always been that way. I graduated from high school in 1973. At that time, women still weren't allowed to fly military aircraft, nor were the service academies accepting women yet. My father, though, was pushing me to do something outrageous. He wanted me to apply anyway, identifying myself as E. Lowry rather than Elaine Lowry. As the child of an Army colonel, and a National Merit Scholarship finalist with a slew of volunteer activities, I would be a shoo-in for a presidential nomination. There was only one problem: the physical training. The most I had ever run was 600 yards in the Presidential Fitness Test. My high school had no female sports teams, and fitness for girls and women—running, gym workouts, exercise classes—hadn't come into fashion yet. I chickened out, much to his disappointment.

That disappointment stung. But I knew I couldn't have met the physical challenge; I was simply unprepared. I vowed that if I ever had a daughter, she would be ready to do whatever she wanted.

Life is full of second chances, and I got one when four years later I found myself in Air Force ROTC working toward a commission as I pursued an MBA. After successfully completing six weeks of field training—one of eight women to make it through (we started out as thirty-six)—the commissioning physical exam twenty months later yielded some puzzling test results. Ultimately, my dreams of active-duty service were dashed when I was diagnosed with an autoimmune condition that prevented me from receiving my gold bars as a second lieutenant one month before commissioning.

What a terrible disappointment. I had worked so hard to reach my goal, and now I had to regroup. I was lucky to have a wise commanding officer to counsel me as I did my separation paperwork. "Never think that this training was wasted," he said. "You have become a better-informed citizen and someone who truly understands the role of the military and the demands of military service. Everyone in your sphere of influence will be changed because you completed this training."

As my children, one by one, headed off for military service, I found myself frequently recalling his words.

When I tell folks I have four military kids, they automatically assume they are all boys. "No, there is a rose among the thorns," I usually say with a smile.

Don't get me wrong. I love being the mother of sons. They are an adventure from morning to night, and thanks to them, for years I inhabited a wonderfully chaotic world of dropped socks and few words with lots of fishing and food in between. Once we had two boys, I begged Courtney for the chance to try for a girl, and when she arrived, I was elated. What would she be like, this new gift from God who would counter the overwhelmingly male environment of my household? There was no way of telling, of course. I knew at least one of my boys would most likely end up in the military; Eric had declared he would be Top Gun at age four. Amazingly enough, today he does fly the F/A-18, a newer version of Top Gun's jet. And once Brendan came along—well, even though when he was a teenager he said he wasn't going to join the military, as a little guy he did have the most extensive collection of plastic army men east of the Mississippi, and by age six he knew every word of dialogue in the movie *The Longest Day.* But Katrina—as determined as she was to not ever be one-upped by her brothers, I have to admit I did not see military service in her future.

That is not to say I didn't realize that she possessed all the qualities of a stellar officer. We military mothers often recognize something different in our daughters early on. As they come of age and head toward military service, their choice catches some of us by surprise, but upon reflection we see how the clues to their future were there all the time. My good friend Melinda told me, "As I look back on it, I could see the soul of a warrior in my daughter from a very young age. She always wanted to do the right thing, and it's been a privilege to watch her discover her talents and gifts over the years.

"After her junior year of high school, she attended the Naval Academy Summer Seminar and came home filled with excitement. She had been screamed at for a week, and done all these horrible sounding things, like push-ups in the river, and she loved it. She saw the greater purpose in all of it. It was exciting for me to see her so energized, but also somewhat mysterious. I had no understanding of this new world she was entering. It was like she was speaking a whole new language. She might as well have been going to Hogwarts."

Georgia, a mom I met on the listserv, also recognized that warrior spirit in her daughter early on. "From the time my daughter was an infant she had a special type of focus that was different from my other children. That focus was apparent in the dedication and the work ethic that led to her excel academically and to become a re-cruited athlete. I can now see that she was meant for this life."

Denise is another friend I met through the listserv. She knew her daughter was headed toward the military when her daughter told her, on September 11, 2001, at the age of thirteen, that she was go-ing to serve her country. "After she finished her somber resolution, she went on to tell me in the very next sentence where she wanted to be buried. I recall the hair standing out on my neck at those words and my response: 'Honey, mommies don't want to talk about things like that on a day like today. But if that is what you really feel you want to do, I will support you.'"

Once it's actually time to go, though, the mother-daughter fare-wells can be brutal. Our pride and our tears come in equal mea-sure. "The hardest and most heart-wrenching day of my entire life was the day before I was to take my older daughter to the Naval Academy," Regina, a fellow Marine mom recalled. "My family is in-credibly close-knit. We have family dinners each evening, share our stories from the day, and laugh together. The day before we were to drive to Maryland, I was with my daughter in her room helping her to pack the very few belongings that she would be taking with her. Suddenly she stopped and looked at me and said that she didn't want to go. She had tears in her eyes as she asked me how she could leave me and her daddy and her family and home. It was all she'd ever known and all she loved in the world. I wanted to say, STAY! DON'T LEAVE! I WILL MISS YOU SO MUCH! And yet I must have had some hidden reserve of strength deep in my heart, for I heard these words leave my lips: 'You have to go.' I told her that if she stayed, she would never know what awesomeness lies within her. She would never know what greatness was waiting to come out. This was her moment. This was her chance. She couldn't live her life wondering *what if.* So I said, 'Go.' And she knew she had to do just that. Then I reached out and I hugged her. And she hugged me. And we cried silently and hugged each other for what seemed like an eternity, never speaking a word because we knew in that moment that we were saying goodbye to how life was. It was the end of our world as we knew it and the beginning of something amazingly incredible, with adventures only a few would ever know."

When Katrina accepted her appointment to the Naval Academy, Courtney and I were filled with pride. But as proud as I was, there was a part of me that *hated* the thought of losing my girl. In the man's world that is our home, she was the ally who enjoyed the things that I did. I could count on her to be my sidekick on shopping expeditions and creative pursuits. And more importantly, she was a kindred spirit, someone who knew how I felt without my saying it aloud. How could I let her go? How could I cope with the idea of her at the point of the spear?

I couldn't say no to her, though. Not only had her father and grandfather and two brothers served, but so had I. And so had my mom. So even though there was a war on, how could I possibly deny her the opportunity to follow her dreams? I had many concerns that are shared by other mothers of daughters, though, some easy to talk about and some held close to the heart, difficult to articulate or to share.

Will my girl fit in? Most mothers whose daughters contemplate military service find themselves asking this question again and again, most often silently. *Will she be accepted by her male peers? What about all the physical and psychological challenges that come with living in a male-dominated world? And what about those headlines about the harassment that may affect my daughter as she pushes into alpha-male territory?*

Later we may wonder about how to cope with the nature of the roles our daughters may be asked to assume as the front lines become fuzzy and the nature of war changes. We may wonder about the fallout from deployments and how it will affect our daughters and their families, and if the repercussions young women experience are any different than the repercussions young men live with. We may wonder if our daughters' military experiences will change them forever in a way that is not good.

But most of us can't even begin to contemplate these big, difficult questions when our daughters initially enter the military. First we have to come to grips with letting them go, abruptly and painfully, and allowing them to move far beyond any realm where we might protect them and into the rough-and-tumble-testosterone-charged male-dominated environment that still is the hallmark of military training.

The shock of the physicality of their new world begins in basic training. For many women, adapting to the incredibly competitive, physical nature of military training is in direct conflict with old ideas of acceptable and appropriate female behavior. We spend years teaching our children, especially girls, not to hit each other, and then suddenly they're commanded to forget all of their socialization and knock the living daylights out of each other. Every fall, when plebes must take wrestling and boxing, my inbox fills up with complaints from mothers about how difficult it is for their daughters to perform in these classes. Little boys grow up tussling with each other but girls, not so much, and these forms of combat are sheer torture for most of the females. So are the mud pit challenges, where trainees must try to slug the stuffing out of each other. But as confronting as these activities are, it's essential that our girls hold their own, for the ability to keep up becomes a gauge of their worthiness as a potential team member.

(For the record, not all girls find the combat classes challenging. One mother told me that some of her daughter's friends got really angry at her because she hit them so hard in boxing class. After further probing, the plebe said, "Of course I hit them hard. I want an A!")

More than worrying about the physicality of the training, though, we moms worry—in fact, the whole family worries—about whether or not our daughters are going to be accepted by the men in their units. As Georgia's daughter was contemplating attending the Naval Academy, Georgia's father-in-law, a Navy grad himself, had serious reservations about it, mostly centered around his granddaughter fitting into such a male environment.

But in Georgia's heart she knew it was the right place for daughter. "With her black-and-white view of the world and her mission focus it seemed a great fit. She understood that she was taking the path less traveled, and she prepared herself physically and mentally for what she knew would be a tough road ahead. Initially, she loved it and she thrived. She was not prepared, though, for some of the challenges above and beyond the daily grind that were faced by female mids. The 'ship, shipmate, self' concept that is drilled into all plebes during Plebe Summer was just that for some of the male plebes—a concept. My daughter had to learn to adjust her expectations to the reality of life in a community. She had to accept that Navy ideals are sometimes in sharp contrast to human nature. It was a painful lesson to learn."

Over time, Georgia's father-in-law's reservations about his granddaughter's service were replaced by enthusiastic support. "He knows that his time at USNA was very different from his granddaughter's time at the Boat School," Georgia told me, "but he recognizes that the motivation that led him to the Academy many years ago is not all that different from his granddaughter's motivation: they both wanted to pursue an excellent education and to serve their country. He is now as proud as a peacock."

Most mothers of military daughters share concerns about harassment even if we don't speak them out loud. While none of my friends' daughters have experienced the headline-grabbing variety, nor have any of Katrina's friends (that we know about), there is no question that our daughters must both prove themselves and protect themselves in ways that aren't an issue for our sons.

Having been through a military training myself, I tried to prepare my daughter for what she might experience along the way, just like any mother whose daughter was venturing out of the safe harbor of home for the first time. The *Welcome to the Military* speech I gave to Katrina—and have given to a number of other young women, as well—goes something like this:

As a woman your most important job is to be prepared. Expect to have to earn your credibility as a warrior. You should be strong physically; like it or not, women are judged by their ability to perform physically. If you can hold your own in a physical challenge, your standing will be elevated among your male peers. First climb the rope, do the sit-ups, and run the mile, and then they will pay attention to how well you can lead.

Keep your working relationships on a professional level. Do not date your peers. Allow people to see you first as a fellow soldier or sailor or airman—as a teammate—not as a female. Do not ever use your sexuality as a tool; rely instead on your professional knowledge, your skills, and your brains to help you get ahead. Guard your heart and maintain appropriate boundaries. In other words, use good judgment—the same good judgment and common sense you would use on a college campus or in the traditional working world. If you are in a situation where you need help, your peers can be great assets if you have cultivated good relationships with them. But that respect has to be earned, and as a woman you will have to put forth extra effort to earn it. You may say, "That's not fair," and maybe it isn't. But life is what you make it.

Over the years, I've had a number of conversations with young female officers in my quest to understand what military life is like for women today, and I've been reminded that one of the main challenges faced by women in uniform is the same challenge that any member of a minority faces in a group—one bad apple spoils how the rest of the fruit in the barrel is perceived. Everything a girl does is just noticed more, which makes perfect sense when you think about it, because even with hair pulled back and dressed in fatigues, girls look different. So any given female's behavior is noticed more than any given male's.

"Often there's a perception that this Barbie in camo just won't be able to hack it," one Air Force officer told me. "Which is exactly how I liked it. When I did more push-ups, finished the 10k faster, or could handle pressure with a calm cool head, it was noticed . . . and respected. And really, that's all that 99 percent of the men I've worked with wanted—someone who was competent and could pull their own weight. Someone that could be a comrade-in-arms and not a burden. But that doesn't come without A LOT of effort. Challenging yourself to always pass the men's physical training standards isn't easy, but it certainly quiets the peanut gallery that whines about the different standards for men and women. Working tirelessly to build up your upper body strength to climb that rope may seem impossible, but slapping the top board is definitely worth it. And gaining the confidence (or just learning to fake it) to give orders, lead, and inspire in challenging situations seems hard, but competence and confidence are what your brothers- and sisters-in-arms are yearning for.

"Choose to be your best," this captain told me. "Choose to work doubly hard. Not because you need to prove yourself, but because adversity and strife sharpen the sword. They make you a better solider, sailor, marine, or airman. Your best is what the nation has called you to be, and it is what your brethren in arms deserve. When my helicopter landed during a mortar attack on our FOB, none of the young soldiers on the helicopter seemed to care that I was a female and had a bun of hair under my helmet. They did seem to care that I was able to get them off and to a bunker quickly and safely. A competent leader is all anyone really wants."

Amen.

There's no doubt that meeting the highest standards of physical fitness, working tirelessly to sharpen skills and increase knowledge, and developing respect-based peer relationships will help our daughters move forward in their military careers. Dana, a Marine mom, offered additional no-nonsense advice when we discussed the learnings her daughter had shared with her.

"My girl was deployed to Afghanistan with a special operations team for nine months," she told me. "Thirty commandos, my daughter, her sergeant, and a female translator. She told me that one thing she learned from her time in the military was to NEVER, EVER go into one of the guys' rooms to chat. Even if the door was left open. Even if someone else was in the room, too. 'It isn't worth the word getting around that you are a slut or easy,'" her daughter told her. (Yes, this sounds harsh.) "For her entire deployment my daughter held herself to this rule," Dana told me. "Don't think she didn't interact or have fun with the guys. Her deployment photo album has dozens of shots of bonfires, barbecues, and nighttime laughter in the makeshift workout gym that the entire group shared. Her sergeant, however, by nature a friendly person, spent time in the room of one of the guys. They had the door open. Nothing happened. It was totally platonic and public, yet the rumors spread unfairly. My daughter saw what happened to her sergeant and never allowed it to happen to her."

The first few years of my daughter's service were a blur. She made it through her entire Plebe Summer without ever dropping out of a run or a physical training. And for all my worries about her fitting in, having grown up with boys, she was used to them—how they think, how they act, how they talk. Her company mates became a new crop of brothers. She had outstanding experiences, including a summer internship with NASA astronauts and a semester at the Air Force Academy as part of an exchange program. It was there that she met her husband-to-be, Preston, who is now an Air Force Huey helicopter pilot. Ultimately she ended up cross-commissioning to the Air Force and becoming an F-16 propulsion engineer. I was thrilled and relieved that it was a not a deployable position. Eric was preparing to deploy, and Jordan was close behind him. At least I wouldn't have to worry about Katrina.

So when I got the news, ten months after her graduation from the Naval Academy, that she was being sent to Afghanistan, I was flabbergasted. Not only was she being sent to Afghanistan as a second lieutenant, but she was going *alone*. She'd be doing a logistical analysis of all the air traffic control equipment operated by the military in Afghanistan, which necessitated traveling to air bases all around the vast country. *Why alone?* I kept asking myself. *What was the point of that?* She would be the first of her classmates to be deployed there. Her Marine counterparts hadn't even finished their training yet. I was stunned and frightened. Terrified, actually.

The week before she left, I visited her in Oklahoma. She was ready. Her farm-girl background had prepared her well; she was used to roughing it in difficult conditions. Chasing a bull back into the pasture was a physical and mental challenge she had overcome time and again. Living in a tent? She had slept out on the hay wagon alone at night. And hunting and target practice made her very comfortable with weapons, so she had excelled at her shooting qualifications. She was excited to see the country she had heard so much about. And, like any member of the military, she was ready to "get into the game." I, on the other hand, was wishing she could do her part from the good old USA. She wisely pointed out to me that it was not fair for others to go and for her to stay home. I said goodbye with a heavy heart.

I learned to cope. I had no choice. She moved from base to base, from Kabul to Kandahar to Bagram and beyond. There was a helicopter ride into Ghazni, which is also known as Rocket City because of the constant shelling that rains down on the base from the surrounding mountains. She rode in convoys and stayed in all manner of temporary housing. More than once she was asked what she was doing there alone as a second lieutenant, a question I continued to ask as well.

There were some high points, including the time she was allowed to meet up with her dad, who was working as the director of training for Safi Airways and was based in Kabul. A picture of the two of them grinning from atop an Afghan pony cheered me up whenever I looked at it. There were also some low points. One morning I was on my way to church when she e-mailed. I had pulled the car over and was enjoying a few minutes reading her e-mail when I got to the sentence: "I have to get to the bunker Mom. We're being rocketed." End of e-mail. I spent the next hour in the church parking lot in tears. Finally she was back on e-mail promising never to do that again. I think I aged ten years in those sixty minutes.

After four interminable months, my daughter returned to the United States. My best friend and I drove to Baltimore to meet her upon her arrival. Her flight ended up being six hours late, but there we were, bleary-eyed, when the plane landed at four A.M. Other returnees who made it through the entryway before she did knew who we were waiting for because we were holding a huge poster with her picture on it, and they gave us updates. "She's picking up her weapons now," or "She's right behind me." And then there she was, my beautiful girl, coming through those double doors with a big smile. It was better than the day she was born.

But Baltimore was just a stop en route to Oklahoma, where her husband was also waiting to welcome her. In the eight hours before her next flight out, she told us many stories, including several that involved close calls that she had kindly neglected to mention while she was there. Her B hut, where she lived in Kandahar, had been destroyed a day after she left that base. In Ghazni, she missed being injured by a rocket strike because at the last minute she had to run back to her hut to retrieve her body armor. The people she was walking with were both hit and seriously injured. I could handle hearing the truth because she was there in my arms.

There are so many things to worry about when it's your daughter in combat boots. We worry about her fitting into a very male environment. We worry about the physical challenges, and about her safety. And we also worry about the time she will be called away from her own babies to deploy far away. Katrina sat in a bunker in Ghazni with a young mom whose own mother was now caring for that soldier's two-month-old baby daughter. The public affairs officer I met when I was living in Kabul had left behind a two-year-old and a three-year-old for six months. My heart breaks for those mothers; I can't imagine the pain of leaving my little ones. When I was given long-term care papers that designated me as the guardian in case both my son-in-law and daughter are both deployed at the same time, I felt like weeping. Worrying about my daughter is hard enough. Worrying about her worrying about leaving her babies behind? I try not to think about it. Yet families all over the United States face this difficult reality every day.

And we worry about the toll that combat, or being in a combat zone, takes on our daughters. The psychological stress of seeing so much pain and suffering seems to affect women in a different way than it affects men.

Dana's daughter, who deployed with a female engagement team, was embedded for eight months in a tribal culture in which the woman's only role was to produce children for the tribe. It was a jarring, even shocking, experience for her. "It was long enough for me to fear my daughter has been changed forever," Dana confides. "I sense a rough edge that comes to the fore even in our conversations. She can snap at me or make a comment that cuts to my heart, completely unaware that she has done so. I know this behavior is a shield that she has had to acquire, having lived in a completely male-dominant environment for so long, both in terms of the tribe and the military."

As I explored ways to help my daughter and other mothers' daughters deal with the trauma of war zone experiences, I discovered that current research suggests that female veterans may be more resilient than male veterans, as long as they have not been impacted by military sexual trauma, or MST, and as long as they have not been injured in combat. (In contrast, women in the military who have experienced previous sexual trauma—presumably primarily MST, which is defined as sexual assault or harassment—or who have been injured in combat are estimated to be at least twice as likely as male members of the military to suffer from posttraumatic stress disorder, or PTSD, and probably more.)

Researchers attribute this resiliency to the tendency of women to be both more open to talking about their feelings and the things that they have seen and experienced, and more willing to get help. As military mothers, we must remember to keep communication lines open and listen even when our daughters are sharing things that are hard to hear or, at the other end of the spectrum, seem unimportant. Sometimes little details, details that seem completely mundane to us, have great meaning to our children.

One of my friends, a Marine mother, shared the following story with me. I listened gratefully, for I knew I could have made the same mistake that she did.

"I had never been to Camp Lejeune before," she told me. "I was in the car on base with my daughter as we drove through many areas to our ultimate destination. It was late fall and I saw a lot of tall, skinny trees and bushes that had lost their leaves and simply looked scrawny to me. I had heard about these trees and shrubs from my daughter many months earlier, and I opened my big fat mouth and said 'These trees and bushes don't look that awful.' To which, in legitimate anger, my girl responded: 'MOM, you don't know what you are talking about. Try hiking through them in the dark, with no clear idea of where you are going. Try having to push through brush, spiders, bugs, and branches that snap back at you as you are bitten and scratched in the blackness. Try it in wet boots as your feet swell. THESE FIELDS ALMOST BROKE ME!'

"My daughter went silent suddenly. Clearly she was reliving in her mind some awful memories. I realized I had no idea *what* she had experienced during her training. That I will never understand what she endured. I immediately apologized, taking full responsibility for saying such a dumb thing. And my beautiful daughter forgave me."

My own daughter has told me stories that made me want to cover my ears and shout "Stop! I can't listen anymore!" But I've hung on, and we've both sobbed through it, and it seems to me that saying tough stuff out loud has helped her. I, too, have some memories from Afghanistan that tumble out in tears, sometimes when I least expect it. When I can let these memories flow rather than trying to stuff them, I know it's healthier for me. I think this advice also holds true for our sons, but it's my experience that sons are not as apt to talk about the dark things that continue to upset them, even when we try to offer them opportunities to do so. This doesn't mean, of course, that we should ever stop giving them openings to talk about the disturbing things they've seen and lived through; on the contrary, we need to give them as many opportunities as we can without making them uncomfortable.

Our daughters may need help in decompressing, relaxing, and regaining their softer sides once they return from deployments or tough duty assignments. This is especially true if they are mothers, too. We may need to remind them gently that reentry is not necessarily an automatic and easy process, and that there is no shame in getting some transition help. Research regarding the impact of female deployment on families continues, and the military is trying to provide more resources, but at the end of the day, you—warrior military mom that you are—need to do what you have always done for your daughter: keep talking, and keep her talking. Be there if you can—whether it is in person or via FaceTime or Skype. And keep advocating for more services to help our military children's children. They are our grandbabies and the future of our nation.

The urge to protect our girls can overwhelm us at times. On those difficult days, we have to work especially hard to remember that our daughters are stronger than steel; they wouldn't have made it this far if they weren't. They have proven themselves in the mud and the dust. They are accomplished and they are prepared.

And we moms are, too. We can stand strong behind the young women we've raised. Our job is to keep the home fires burning and not weigh our daughters down with concerns about the toll their deployments, or any of their other challenges, take on us. It's an important job, stoking those home fires, and one we have to take seriously. So push those pink tulle memories to the background. Think about the most important lesson we taught our daughters as they were growing up—*girls can do anything*—and know that it applies to women, too. It applies to us. We are tough. Just like our ballerinas in combat boots.

Oh, the Places They'll Go

Kindergarten graduation. Shiny faces, big smiles, and paper mortarboards atop mop tops and crew cuts. I know you remember it, too. As the pixies walk up to receive their kindergarten "diplomas," they announce their plans for the future. I wanna be: a fireman, a nurse, a teacher, a princess, a doctor, Top Gun, a football player, a turkey farmer, a ballerina, an astronaut.

Big dreams for little people. Big dreams for moms and dads, too.

And yes, Courtney and I dreamed big, just like so many of you. The message we always tried to communicate to our children was *The sky's the limit! You can do or be anything!* So when Katrina received the Dr. Seuss book *Oh, the Places You'll Go* on the auspicious occasion of completing kindergarten, we knew it was the perfect gift for her. It was as if our family ethos had been translated into rhymes and pictures and bound between the covers of that book.

Night after night, our children clambered up on the couch next to me, and we read through all the possibilities. Maybe they would become doctors. Maybe they would find their niches in boardrooms. They were good arguers, so maybe one would end up in a courtroom. And how about "Brendan Brye for a touchdown!"?

We didn't let the scary stuff in life stop us, no way. Because the message of the book rang loud and clear: You can do it. It doesn't matter where you start. There will be setbacks, but you can make your own destiny.

But what happens when your children's big dreams diverge from your big dreams? What if the places they'll go are not classrooms or boardrooms or operating rooms, but battlefields, submarines, and fighter jets? When the future includes tours of duty in Afghanistan, Iraq, Liberia, and Djibouti?

Sure, some military moms see signs of a future soldier from their child's early days. "Ivan was intrigued with anything and everything military," an Army mom named Melissa remembers. "He always wanted to go to the Memorial Day parade to see the soldiers march by. Every Halloween his costume was the same thing: he was a soldier. We did not go to Toys 'R' Us to shop for it, we went to Army Navy surplus. I kept thinking it was a phase he would grow out of. But now he's twenty-eight and in Special Forces and he's living his dream. I guess you could say he never did grow out of it."

Another friend told me her son had loved ships for as long as she could remember. "Some kids wanted rubber duckies in the bathtub. We had submarines. And we had different types of submarines. By the time Wayne was six, he could tell the difference between a frigate and a destroyer. Now he's in the Navy, and I still don't know the difference. I don't know where it came from, but I guess he was truly called to the sea. No one in my family was ever in the Navy. In fact, no one was ever in the military. We don't even live near an ocean for heaven's sake. It's a mystery to me."

Once our kids choose this somewhat mysterious life of military service, the world we know changes in some amazing ways. I'm not just talking about the fact that our kids enter a new world of strange protocols, intense physical training, and top secret missions. I'm talking about the fact that the physical world actually expands—or at least it seems like it does. "I got a call from Bhutan the other day," a Navy mom named Lynn said. "I am ashamed to admit it, but I didn't know where Bhutan was. I didn't even know if the country was friend or foe," she continued somewhat sheepishly. "I am assuming friend, or my son wouldn't have told me he was there."

When our loved ones are deployed all over the globe, geography becomes personal. My father deployed to Vietnam in November of 1962, and right before he left he gave us a Peter, Paul, and Mary album featuring the song "Puff the Magic Dragon." In my mind, I equated that song's mythical Land of Honah Lee with Vietnam, so the grainy pictures of soldiers and helicopters I saw on the news confused me; they didn't fit in with my vision of the magical land where I had situated my dad. At that point, life for me was still a mix of school, Girl Scouts, and playing with my siblings, but it wasn't long before I learned to locate Vietnam on a map, and Cambodia and Laos, too.

Years later when my own young children were running around the backyard, the Gulf War directed my attention to the countries of the Middle East. Iraq, Kuwait, and Saudi Arabia became the subject of the evening news, countries that I learned about and read about. And of course, after September 11th, Iraq came into even sharper focus, and Pakistan and Afghanistan were now part of the picture, too.

From time to time, I look back on those first two months of Eric's plebe year at the Naval Academy before the World Trade Center buildings came crashing down. During those simpler days (although they didn't feel simple at the time; I was still adjusting to life as a military mom), I thought I knew where my military son might be headed upon commissioning. Perhaps Okinawa? Or maybe

Italy? Italy would be a beautiful place to be stationed for a while, I thought. After growing up during the Cold War years and coming of age during Vietnam and watching Eastern Europe explode, I should have known better than to try to predict things. But I didn't. And I certainly never imagined that I, too, would one day end up living in a battle-beleaguered country for the better part of a year.

Today's military family members—parents, children, spouses, siblings—can tell you exactly where Afghanistan is situated on the map. We can tell you where Helmand and Ghazni and Kabul are located. We can distinguish between the climates of Kandahar and Jalalabad, and we know the common ports near the Straits of Hormuz. We know that Manas, Kyrgyzstan, is the place of entrance and exit for those serving in Afghanistan; I cried when my daughter landed there and celebrated when she flew away. Geography *is* personal.

Most military parents can also tell you about Asia, where two of my sons have been deployed. Who knew that there were islands being claimed by both China and Japan, and that the United States patrols that area in the air and on the water? And when the tsunami hit Japan in 2011, and one son had just landed at Midway, I had no idea that he was in a region that might be affected by that devastating natural disaster. And what about North Korea, which continues to be in a constant state of chaos?

And then there's Libya. Although I wasn't supposed to know it at the time, my instincts were right when I surmised that one of my boys was flying reconnaissance operations over that country during the Arab Spring uprisings.

Oh, the places they will go. Who can imagine? My world has gotten bigger with each deployment. I've become exceedingly well versed in the cultures, the politics, and the climates of countries I'd once barely heard of. And now in this turbulent world I look to the evening news again. Will I soon be learning all I can about South Sudan, Syria, Mali, and the Paracel Islands? Will these be the future homes of my military kids? Time will tell.

"When David joined the Air Force, I never thought he would end up in Africa," Julie, a fellow military mom from Ohio, told me. "None of us knew much about that continent. Then we got a letter that said, 'Mom, once I got used to how different things were, I realized it was really the same. Kids are kids, families are families. Moms want the same things for their kids. Somehow it made me feel less homesick and better about being away from my own family.' It made me feel better about him being there, too," Julie concluded.

And it makes me feel better, too. It's true that some deployments leave our kids feeling like they're in somewhat familiar territory, and others leave them feeling like they're on a different planet. Often we can predict which will be which; sometimes we cannot. It's hard to know.

What I do know after all these years of growing up in the military and now being a military parent is that the front is ever expanding. And whether it's the Cold War, Vietnam, the Gulf War, or the War on Terror, someone needs to be standing watch. And those someones happen to be our loved ones.

I would not be completely honest if I didn't confess that some deployments are harder than others. The ones shrouded in secrecy, when I don't know where my kids are, drive me crazy. There are a lot of other parents and loved ones in that boat, and I take comfort in knowing I am not alone.

And yet no matter how much comfort I derive from that fact, no matter how much I've let go, I still grasp for some shred of information to hold onto, as do most military family members. So we continue our geography lessons on the Internet, trying to understand more about the bigger world in which our family members serve. We find new recipes for care package cookies that will withstand heat or high humidity. We do what we can to support our loved ones. And yes, sometimes we just shut off the evening news and focus on memories of baby days when they were safely in our arms or sweet childhood days in the backyard. You remember. The days when we knew where they were and the world was a smaller and much simpler place.

Backpack

*A*s the mother of a small herd of children, I've purchased my fair share of backpacks. For some reason, finding just the right one for each of my kids was the highlight of our back-to-school shopping every year. Eric's favorite color was black, and for six years he wore black to school every day. We called him Johnny Cash. Naturally, the adjustment to wearing a black uniform at the Naval Academy was seamless, and the plebes were even issued black backpacks.

Jordan preferred a classic, well-functioning pack. He was very organized, and his backpack choice reflected that. Katrina, on the other hand, went for Big is Beautiful. She always carried a lot of stuff home. In fact, she had one of the first rolling backpacks at her school after I determined that a forty-pound load was a little excessive. And Brendan? He was easy. Anything involving the GI Joe look would do.

I began wearing my own backpack when my children joined the military. I wasn't even aware that I had put it on until I found myself feeling so weighed down that at times it was hard to put one foot in front of the other. Each problem that one of my kids told me about became a brick that I added to my pack. Roommate issues? Add a brick. Academic woes? Add a brick. Laid up with a 104-degree fever and no mother there to wipe his brow or spoon soup into her mouth? Add a couple of bricks. The inevitable "It's not fair!" complaint (and often it's not), add a concrete block.

After a time, though, I noticed that a funny thing was happening. It seemed that just the act of venting to me made my kids' loads lighter while mine got heavier and heavier. While I was getting a backache from bearing their burdens, they were solving their own problems and moving on. Just like we want them to do. They simply forgot to tell me that their problems had been resolved, and so I trudged around with this weighty load much longer than they did. I thought it was my responsibility to worry for them. It was something I could *do*. Odd as it may sound, it was a way to keep them close to me.

"Every letter my daughter wrote was a litany of complaints. She hated *everything*," Anita, a listserv mom, told me. "'Mom, I made the biggest mistake of my life. I can't stand anything about this place,' she'd write. My husband finally said he wasn't going to let me read her letters. When it came time for the first phone call, I was prepared to go pick her up. I was sure she was quitting, and I was already devastated. I was shocked when she didn't even remember writing all of those negative things. 'Oh mom, I was just temporarily out of my mind,' she said. Out of her mind?! She almost put me out of mine!"

The loads most of us moms shoulder in those first years of our kids' military service are very much the same. We listen to complaints about grueling schedules, stupid rules, and things not being fair. We learn about what we can and cannot do (mostly the latter) and how we can and cannot help our kids (100 percent the latter). "When things happened that were just not fair and I could do nothing about it—boy, I carried that brick around with me for a while. In fact, I carried it around so long it was worn smooth, like a worry rock," said Jennifer, a Navy mom, "I just wanted to go up there and kick some shins, but my son needed to handle it."

A lot of us can identify with that feeling completely.

But what about the bigger bricks, and the bigger worries? The ones that come when your child is deployed? The ones that sneak up on you when you're in the grocery store and someone asks about him and you dissolve in tears because there's been no word in months and you don't know where he is? I hate that damn "on a need to know basis" protocol. As far as the military is concerned, mothers don't ever need to know. But of *course* we need to know. These are our sons and daughters we're talking about. Not knowing where our kids are or what they are doing weighs very, very heavily on us.

Samantha, an Army mom, wrote, "I feel I am losing my son. There is so much of his world he cannot tell me about. I don't hear from him for months at a time, and when I do, he cannot tell me almost anything. He's like a stranger. I knew he would be away physically, but I was not prepared for this kind of separation."

Or what about when there's breaking news in the part of the world where you're pretty sure she's stationed—terrible news—and your heart stops? And then it happens again the next day, and the next. Sandra, an Army mom, opted to throw off the burden of that brick from her backpack by no longer watching the news. "After all, most of it is wrong," she said. "They'll say there's been a helicopter crash in Kabul, but it's actually in Herat. Well, there's a big difference between the two—a big difference to me, anyway. I need to do what I can to protect myself and my heart." In the words of a Special Forces mom: "I just have to let it all go. Dump it all. Not think about it. I immerse myself in things I enjoy. I volunteer. I try to make my immediate world a better place."

Let me tell you something that you may not want to hear: you can't absorb all of your son's or daughter's hurts, anxieties, frustrations, and worries. I know you want to. I know you think that by adding this brick to your pack, you are unburdening your child. But the truth is that lugging these issues around is not helping your loved ones. So here's your challenge: dump some of those bricks. You may not feel able to get rid of all that weight at once, but you can start. If you're able to let go of the idea that you can change it or fix it, whatever "it" is, you will immediately feel that your burden has been lightened.

And while you're reevaluating what you're carrying around in your pack, you might also consider adding to it. Something lightweight, of course, something that doesn't take up a lot of space. And something that you want there, not something that's been foisted on you. Me, I've added a pair of knitting needles and some yarn.

Knitting, for me, is a wonderful way to at least temporarily dispel worries and concerns, a skill that any military parent needs to master. I first picked up a set of size 10 needles when Brendan was participating in high school athletics. What else do you do when you're confined to the bleachers as your son plays his heart out on JV with the hope of getting in for varsity? Let your guts twist up in disappointment when he doesn't make it? Snarl at the referee when you really want to throttle the coach? I picked up my short, pointy needles and started knitting furiously. Little did I know what an essential military mom skill I would be developing.

Now knitting is my link to sanity, my silent supplication when my children are in harm's way, my tears when a company mate is lost. I turn my frantic thoughts into stitches, each one becoming a prayer.

While my needles click away, I feel a new affinity for all those women in World War I and World War II who knit and rolled bandages. The mindless act of making neat stitches, combined with meditation and prayers for those I love, helps me stay somewhat peaceful. This world is a scary place. And since my children have chosen to be in the middle of all that danger, at least I can make sure they'll have something warm to take with them. At least I can make sure that their babies will be wrapped in protection that I have provided.

Eric once commented on Facebook, "You can tell when mom has someone deployed. Knitting production goes way up." Yes, it does! The good news is that I am really improving as a knitter thanks to all these deployments.

Knitting needles and yarn in the backpack notwithstanding, I will always be looking for ways to lighten my own load and the loads of other military moms, and there's a story Eric told me from his time at The Basic School (TBS) that never fails to help me stand a little taller and breathe a little easier. Required of every Marine Corps Officer, TBS provides the training necessary to serve as a rifle platoon commander no matter what one's job in the Corps. If chosen as an aviator, an officer must still learn hand-to-hand combat. Headed toward a job in Supply? Finance? The Military Police? It doesn't matter; all officers must learn to operate in combat, and most importantly, to lead enlisted Marines.

Among other things, TBS training requires a lot of time in the field under difficult conditions learning combat fighting, orienteering, and other essential survival skills. Repeated ruck marches—hikes of increasingly long distances carrying rucks, or backpacks, filled with heavy gear—are part of the drill.

Quantico in the summer is hot and muggy. It's no picnic to march in full gear through brush and swampland for miles and miles. As the Marines trudge one behind the other in a long line, sometimes someone stumbles or hits the wall. And that's when he grabs onto the pack in front of him. In extreme cases, another Marine will carry the faltering Marine's pack so they all make it together.

How do I cope with letting go? Some days are harder than others. On those harder days, I knit, I pray, and I hang onto someone else who has walked the path before me. The band of military mothers and fathers is strong, and its members know the price we all pay to let go time and time again. Other military parents can help you carry your backpack on the days it feels loaded with cement blocks. Whether you find them in person or virtually, or simply know they're out there battling with you in spirit, it's a comfort and a gift to realize that you are not alone. We all need help with our backpacks from time to time. We are all in this together.

You Are
Not Alone

The Sisterhood
and Beyond

$\mathcal{I}$t was the fourth Friday of field training at McConnell Air Force Base in Wichita, Kansas, and I was about to find out if I would be allowed to complete the program or be forced to leave. That year, 1977, was the first year that field training, the ROTC equivalent of boot camp, was coed, and I was one of thirty-six women in a class of several hundred cadets. I had an advantage over most of the other women in that I was twenty-one and had already completed my bachelor's degree, whereas the majority of the other females were several years younger and only partway through college. Though the training was tough, I managed to have fun, too. And now that the statute of limitations has run out, I can confess that yes, I was the ringleader in stealing the Delta Company flag. But the fitness part of the training was my Achilles' heel.

Every Friday we had to perform the Physical Readiness Test, or PRT. We had two minutes to do a prescribed number of push-ups and sit-ups—I can't remember how many after all these years—and then came a timed mile-and-a-half run. I did fine with the push-ups and sit-ups, but that mile-and-a-half trip around the track continued to be my Waterloo. Earlier in the year, in order to lose weight and be eligible for ROTC, I'd started running every night, and once I'd dropped the necessary pounds and knew I'd be attending field training, I'd kept running. But every Friday at McConnell, I'd miss the twelve-and-a-half minute cutoff by just a few seconds. I'd work hard all week and come in under time, and then panic would set in as the Friday run began. It seemed that no matter what I did—deep breathing, visualization; I was willing to try anything—my muscles would turn to rubber and I simply couldn't shave off those last few seconds. I had to pass by the end of week four or I would be sent home.

Each flight (company) ran as a group. On that make-or-break fourth Friday I was the only female left in my flight; all the others had quit ROTC. I took my position on the starting line, and I was already hyperventilating when the pistol sounded. Within seconds I felt my muscles turning to mush, way ahead of schedule, and then an amazing thing happened. The men in my flight closed in around me in a V formation. No one is allowed to touch you as you run, but they got as close as they could, and they started to scream at me.

"What's the matter?! Can't a girl do this? Come on! Don't be a quitter, Lowry! Don't stop! Don't slow down! Come on, *come on*, COME ON!"

They shouted to push me and they shouted to make me mad. And at the same time that my anger ignited an extra spark of adrenaline, the sheer presence of so many bodies around me was like the force of the wind, and I found myself struggling less.

I crossed the finish line with five seconds to spare and my big tough fellow cadets—my band of brothers—surrounded me in a huge group hug, whooping and hollering. I had done it. *We* had done it. At that moment, I knew I would finish the remaining two weeks of the training. I knew that I was not in this experience alone.

Some days I feel like my knees are going to give out and no matter how much I push, I'm struggling. When I'm faced with yet another deployment, another empty chair at a family celebration, another missed call on my cell in the middle of the night; when I feel like I have no more Semper Gumby in me and I just want to give up—that's when I need my V of fellow military moms to circle in around me, close, and say, "C'mon. You've got this. We can *do* this. Just one more step."

There are plenty of other days, though, that I start out of the gate strong, keeping pace with the demands of my crazy life, confident that I *can* do this. On those days, I'm a part of that V, running alongside a fellow mom to encourage her, answering her call in the middle of the night when her fears creep in. And a funny thing happens. When I'm running alongside her, not only does her endurance increase, but so does mine. I forget my pain, my shortness of breath. We all get stronger.

Which brings me to the Sisterhood. The moment your child enlists in the military, you are inducted into the most powerful unofficial sorority in the world: the Sisterhood of Military Moms. This Sisterhood includes moms you can count on for support even if you don't know them personally. Moms you can count on to help out your kids when they're far from home and in need of some attention. Moms who will go visit your kid in the hospital when he's injured in boot camp and you live too far away to get there. Moms who will drop everything to be there for you if you need a serious pep talk—if you've heard, say, a news report about casualties in what could be your daughter's unit and you haven't heard from her in three days and you think you just might lose your mind. Moms who will talk you down off the proverbial ledge and get you to stop hyperventilating until you finally hear something. If the news is good, these mothers will celebrate with you, and if it's not good, they'll huddle in close and take care of you.

Welcome to the Sisterhood. No pledging necessary. Your child has done it for you.

I changed schools and school districts twelve times between kindergarten and eleventh grade, and I hated that "new kid" feeling every time. The loneliness of being a stranger was overwhelming; I didn't know who to trust or how to find my way around. At those times, I wanted nothing more than to stop feeling different. I wanted to wake up in the mornings and recognize the wallpaper and know I was home. I wanted to belong.

But, inevitably, before long, someone asked me to sit at her lunch table. And someone else offered to show me how to find my homeroom. And someone else invited me to join Glee Club. And slowly I found my way around. I recognized faces in the halls and had a place in the cafeteria. And, yes, eventually I'd wake up and recognize the wallpaper. I'd finally moved in spirit, as well as location. I belonged.

Maybe you never experienced that "new kid" feeling; perhaps you grew up in the same house your entire life, like Courtney did, and attended the same school from kindergarten until the day you donned your cap and gown as a senior. But I'm guessing that whether you're used to change or comforting sameness, the day your child joined the military you felt like you'd been teleported to a whole new universe. A new galaxy, even.

Sure, some of us parents have a head start in that new galaxy. We served ourselves or grew up on a post or a base, and that definitely gives us a leg up. But it's a whole lot different to have a spouse or parent in the military, or to serve yourself, than it is to have a child—a child for whom you would literally lay down your life—in the military.

For those who come from the civilian world, well, gosh, fasten yourself in and get ready for liftoff. More than learning a whole new language, you will have to learn a whole new way of *thinking*. This is harder than it sounds. What is logical and appropriate to you, a civilian parent, may not be logical or appropriate in a military context. And your role in your child's life will change. You will have to get used to not being in control, not knowing where your son or daughter is, or perhaps worse, when you do know, wishing that you didn't. It will be a colossal, and sometimes wrenching, adjustment.

But the good news is this: you are not alone.

Consider Denise, a Marine mom who had sent four sons off to college by the time her fifth child, a daughter, was ready to go. Denise knew what it was like to separate from a child, but with her youngest's departure she was now an empty nester, and to make matters just a little harder, her daughter was only seventeen when she left for the US Naval Academy—young enough that Denise still had to sign her forms as the adult guardian. And then Denise and her husband moved in order to be closer to his workplace, leaving her not only without her kids, but without her familiar surroundings and her friends, as well. "When my youngest child left for the Naval Academy, I felt completely and utterly alone," she remembers.

With no kids to care for and in a new community, Denise struggled to feel connected. She and her husband joined a local church, and she started volunteering there, "but that wasn't filling up my empty heart," she wrote. Then she realized that she was less than eight miles from the Marine Corps Air Station Miramar, and so she contacted the Navy Marine Corps Relief Society to see if she could volunteer there. "I spoke to the director and informed her that I was the wife of a USNA alum, and that my daughter was a USNA alum who was now a Marine. The director laughed heartily and echoed back: 'I'm the wife of a USNA grad and my daughter is a Marine Officer!' Instantly I felt less alone."

Denise has been volunteering at the Relief Society faithfully for five years now and frequently gets asked why she volunteers. "For my own mental sanity," she often responds, and then elaborates: "Of course, helping others, especially our military families in need, is immensely rewarding. But I've gained easily as much as I've given in the service of others. Seeing the looks of relief and appreciation on the faces of families in financial need, watching young military moms become pregnant and then proudly show off their children as they grow, getting to know the personal stories of some of our older veterans—these things are gratifying on a daily basis. And then there are the parties we volunteers enjoy together several times a year, and the home-baked treats we share regularly in the break room. I've built a core group of good friends and I'm grateful for every one of them."

Volunteering in a military community has been essential in helping Denise understand the tight-knit military culture that her daughter lives in. When her daughter tore her meniscus—a bad knee injury—in Marine Officer Basic School, a female officer comforted Denise and explained the steps for her daughter's rehab. When her daughter was handpicked for a special operations deployment, Marines who shopped in the store where Denise volunteers explained what her daughter's training and life ahead would be like. When her daughter's deployment date was moved and then moved again—and again—other military wives and moms understood the frustration and stress that those changes cause. "Been there, done that," they would commiserate, and then they'd laugh, and it made the situation easier to bear.

"The military community is a family," Denise asserts with conviction. "And this family understands hardship and challenges and pain and sorrow and is always there to support you. Having been on the receiving end of this kind of loving care, all I can do is give back again and again. It is incredibly satisfying, mentally stimulating, and heart humbling. And every day I am grateful to be a part of this community of proud Americans."

A few years ago, Judy, who has both a son and a son-in-law who are serving, asked young military wives living on a base about two hours from her home in California how she and others could best support them. They responded that they wanted to have parties for their children at Halloween, Christmas, and Easter, but if they were the ones hosting the parties, then they couldn't actually enjoy them with their kids; it was a lot of work, and if their husbands were deployed, it was a double whammy. So Judy organized all the Girl Scout troops and their parents from her church and started making the four-hour round-trip drive with them at the appropriate holiday times so they could host these events. Now the military children get to enjoy holiday parties and Easter Egg hunts with their moms, and along with the chance to feel great about doing something meaningful for others, the Girl Scouts and their parents get an introduction to the military and tours of the base. And in a beautiful what-goes-around-comes-around-kind of way, some members of the military have even been known to give the Girl Scout troops self-defense lessons.

The effort is all worth it, says Judy. "The appreciation shown by the families on base is overwhelming. Helping out like this has allowed me to realize that the sacrifices made by our military families are far greater than what I experience as just 'the mom.'" These experiences, she says, draw everyone together.

And on the days when having both a son and a son-in-law in the military seems like just too much for Judy? "I know for certain that if anything ever happened, my military friends would be there to support me. And I, in turn, will do anything for them if the roles are reversed. This I know beyond the shadow of a doubt."

My membership in the Sisterhood began a few months before Eric's Induction Day, when I first began connecting with other mothers via the listserv. By now, more than a decade later, we have borne the weight of deployments together, become grandparents at more or less the same time, and shared the grief of burying parents. And the number of Sisters in my circle keeps growing. My children shook their heads one year as we traveled through the tiny town of Three Rivers, Montana, and I said, "I know a Navy mom who lives here."

"Where *don't* you know a Navy mom?" one of them asked in wonder.

I met many of my fellow military moms through the USNA-Parents listserv, but it no longer takes a listserv to find the Sisterhood. Facebook groups and places to connect online now exist for every possible subset of military parent. Navy Moms Online, Marine Moms Online, Marine Parents, Air Force Wing Moms, Army Mom Strong—the list goes on and on. When I joined Facebook, I didn't do it just to see my grandkids' pictures—although I must admit that those young ones are quite captivating—but to see my fellow military moms' beautiful grandbabies, and the pictures of their sons' and daughters' homecomings, as well. And where would we be without our smartphones? Technology is how we connect when we suddenly need to say to someone, "I feel like I'm falling."

Of course, we'll always rely on face-to-face meetings, too. We find each other in bathrooms at boot camp graduations and Army–Navy games. I meet fellow military moms in airports as they finish saying goodbye to a son or daughter. They might be wearing an *Army Mom* T-shirt or an *Air Force Mom* cap, or maybe I'm the one wearing an identifying piece of clothing; it doesn't take much to make the connection. And then there are local community groups like the USO or Blue Star Mothers.

Once a child of yours joins the military, you become a Blue Star Mother, and many of us join our local Blue Star chapters to help put together care packages and support our local Reserve and Guard troops in other ways. We march in parades and go to airports for festive homecomings. We also go for homecomings that are the very opposite of festive—those of the fallen—and stand silently holding flags as the hearse pulls away from the airport. Facing our greatest fears, we attend funerals to support Gold Star Mothers, because they need to know that they are not alone. And that extends beyond club boundaries. When one of our sons' or daughters' USNA classmates or company mates or basic training buddies becomes one of the fallen, the Sisterhood shows up then, too—at the church, at the funeral home, to serve punch and offer hugs, to fill the vacuum created by grief with love and kisses and warm embraces. We do whatever we can to remind a stricken mother that she is surrounded by the love of her fellow mothers, because her child is our child, too.

Even in my tiny rural town I am reminded that I am not alone. My up-the-hill neighbor's son just finished boot camp, and together she and I weigh the chances of him getting home for his sister's wedding. The mothers of former students of mine—students who are now serving—stop me in the grocery store to give me updates. We share a bond that those who don't have this bond struggle to understand; because our children are called upon to do hard things, we do not take the future for granted. We hang on tight to family memories and try to savor what we have in the present. Without speaking, we understand this about each other.

There are so many times I have reached out for a helping hand for myself or some practical help for a kid stranded somewhere. One of the most frightening times was on a cold November afternoon when I got a call from Katrina, who was in Colorado doing an exchange semester at the Air Force Academy.

"Mom, I have a big lump on my tongue," she said, somewhat offhandedly. My blood ran cold. As a former medical technologist, I knew enough about potentially bad medical conditions to have an idea of what this might mean. The situation was even more fraught because we had good friends whose nineteen-year-old son had died of cancer of the tongue. I told her to get to the clinic as soon as possible. My anxiety escalated when my stoic daughter called several days later almost in tears. Words like *tumor, surgery,* and *biopsy* were tumbling out of her mouth. I knew what to do. I put the Sisterhood into action.

Within three days Katrina was at Bethesda Naval Hospital, where one of my fellow Navy moms was a physician. While Courtney stayed home with Brendan and Luke, I stayed with this generous Navy mom at her house, and she watched over me, and Katrina, throughout the surgery and recovery process. During those anxious days, Katrina and I were surrounded by the love and support of many fellow military moms. When the biopsy results finally arrived, there was no cancer, nor had the surgery produced any nerve damage that might have caused a permanent speech impediment.

As I sat in the different waiting rooms of the hospital, both before and after our good news, I marveled at all the people around us, many of whom were in much more dire straits than Katrina. There were moms and dads standing by supporting their sons and daughters, and wives supporting husbands, and friends supporting friends. And when I closed my eyes I could almost see the V surrounding me, and see it expanding to surround everyone else in the room, too. "C'mon," said the voices whispering in my ear. "You've got this. We can *do* this. Just one more step."

In those inevitable moments of fear and confusion and anger that seem to go with having a child in the military, I hope you'll remember to reach out to other members of the Sisterhood. If you are an independent, take-charge kind of person not accustomed to looking for support, let alone *requesting* it, asking for help might feel a little uncomfortable at first. But believe me when I say that those of us who feel like part of a community, even if it's an online community, or who feel the support of even just a few others who are going through the same thing, will fare far better on the Emotional Readiness Test that we have to pass with relentless regularity. Sometimes you may *feel* alone, and that is perfectly normal. But please, don't allow yourself to stay in that place too long; loneliness and isolation don't do anybody any good. The Sisterhood—the Band of

Mothers—is always here for you. We've been right where you are. And we will pour you a cup of coffee and you can cry and complain and we won't judge. We'll pat you on the back, and we'll make sure to have plenty of Kleenex on hand. We won't say, "I told you so!" or tell you that your son or daughter has made a terrible decision or make you feel guilty for "allowing" your children to pursue their dreams in the military. We won't criticize you for doubting yourself or feeling bereft, and we won't deny your feelings. We won't tell you your child's service doesn't matter because he or she is not deployed; we know you miss your children whether they are in the continental United States (CONUS) or halfway around the world, and we know that accidents can happen anywhere. And if your child is still in training, we will remind you that one day much sooner than you think, you'll see him or her standing tall, clear-eyed, and full of purpose, and that your heart will practically burst with pride.

We're ready. We're ready for that moment when you feel like you should just give up, that moment when putting one foot in front of the other feels impossible. And if you let us, we will circle around you, support you with encouragement and a little tough love, if necessary, and we will lift your spirits like the force of the wind.

The Biggest Family
in the World

*Y*our military family extends far and wide. One of the great things about having a large, extended family is that you never know when you're going to bump into a distant cousin. Maybe a cousin so distant, in fact, that the two of you have never met—or even heard of each other.

A mother whose daughter went through the Naval Academy after my children graduated told me that the first time she truly understood that she was part of a deeply interconnected community was when her daughter fell very ill during her plebe year. The family had always been extremely close, and the separation had been tough on both the mother and the daughter. And then, sometime in the fall, there was a meningitis outbreak at the Naval Academy, and her daughter had all the symptoms, including sudden high fever, nausea, sore throat, and a horrific headache. She was given IV fluids and medication and was under the vigilant care of Brigade Medical, but her mother, who was five hundred miles away, was beyond terrified.

Thank goodness she shared her fears with a few of her fellow plebe mothers. Over the course of an afternoon she had an inbox full of offers to help. One fellow plebe mom who lived in the area offered to bring the sick young woman homemade chicken noodle soup. Another family offered to take the young woman into their home, once she was well enough, where they would care for her. Others offered prayers and words of comfort. "I simply couldn't believe that so many people offered to help my daughter—someone they had never met—simply because we were all connected by the Naval Academy," this mother told me. "Instantly I stopped feeling alone, and I wasn't as scared. I will never forget how the Navy family picked me up that day and made one mother so far away from her beloved daughter feel that everything was going to be all right. Whenever I hear of a Navy family who needs some loving care, I am quick to do the same. I know how one thoughtful email can make the difference between despair and hope."

I can vouch for the kindness of Navy parents, and I have seen it replicated time and time again in every branch in all kinds of situations. When Eric had strep throat one year at the Naval Academy and couldn't swallow solid food, a local mom took him chicken soup and milkshakes. And when, due to a string of snafus, Katrina was stranded in a seedy bus station at midnight in Denver, one Navy parent got in her car and went to pick her up to keep her safe. She took Katrina home, gave her a comfortable bed and a great breakfast, and transported her back to the bus station the following morning. Mind you, she had never previously met Katrina. But her son was Jordan's company mate, and that meant Katrina was part of her extended family.

In addition to all of the individual military parents out there who find ways to support each other, parent and alumni organizations associated with the various academies also step up to help in touching ways. One extraordinary young man I heard about spent a large portion of his youth in the foster care system and yet somehow was able to achieve the grades and exhibit the leadership necessary to get accepted into the Naval Academy. Talk about determination and resilience; the thought of his strength of will and character humbles me. When he turned eighteen, he "aged out" of the foster care system and literally found himself without a home base. Local alumni became a point of support for him, storing his personal possessions and providing a home address and a place to land. Other parent organizations have paid for plane tickets to enable academy midshipmen to visit ailing parents or for parents who are struggling financially to visit their children during Parents' Weekends.

There are service academy families and graduates all across the country, and there are both active and retired members of all of the branches of the military far and wide, too. This means that almost anywhere you go, you are bound to find a member of your extended community—or he or she is bound to find you. I have a *USNA Mom* license plate and a Naval Academy sticker on my old '98 Suburban. I can't tell you how many times I have returned to my car in a parking lot to find someone waiting to talk to me. I once emerged from a laundromat at an RV park in Texas to find an older gentleman standing patiently by my car. His son was Naval Academy Class of '88 and this proud father wanted to know all about my kids and where they were stationed. "Bravo Zulu," he said ("well done" in military speak) when I told him where everyone was and what they were doing. "Bravo Zulu!"

If you're entirely new to this world—this family—this assumption of a relationship may sound odd. But I love it. I love that someone I meet coming out of a laundromat in a town I've never visited wants to know if my kids are in CONUS or deployed, and if they're deployed, when they're due home. These people don't know me, and they don't know my kids, but as members of the same family, they actually do care. Just like I care about their family members. "We are the biggest family in the world," one military mom observed to me.

Every day there are random acts of kindness directed toward our young servicemen and servicewomen, and that's good to remember if you're a parent worrying about or missing your child. I've heard of people paying restaurant tabs and giving up first class seats for those in uniform. My kids have been on the receiving end of these kindnesses, and so have others we know. I've heard of people offering services without charge. My daughter-in-law, Tonya, for instance, is a wonderful photographer. One year she took Christmas portraits of families who had a parent deployed over the holidays, so that the deployed parent could be surprised by a beautiful new image of his or her family's smiling faces. A mom named Brooke told me that when her son's unit came home from one deployment, restaurants donated food, a DJ offered his talents, and the extended hometown community turned out to make it a joyous celebration in support of the troops and their families.

Simply thanking someone for his or her service can be meaningful, too. When my kids were still in training, it made them uncomfortable to be thanked. "But I haven't done anything yet," they would say to me. I told them to accept the gratitude on behalf of their brother and sisters—literally and figuratively—who were, in fact, on the front lines. "Recognize that those who thank you are showing respect and thanks not just to you, but to all those who have served," I counseled them. "In accepting their appreciation with gratitude, you are allowing them to contribute."

I'll talk to young people in uniform anywhere and everywhere. Airports and airplanes are likely spots to see people in uniform, and I've had many quick chats in waiting areas or baggage claims. If my children are with me they'll roll their eyes and say, "There she goes again." But I love to connect and show young men and women in uniform my appreciation for their service. And I always tell them to call their mothers!

One flight in late 2004 was especially memorable. I noticed ten soldiers from the 101st Airborne were on board, and I had spoken to one of them earlier that day. She and I had talked about how great it would feel to get a hot shower at home—one of the little things that become so meaningful when you go without. I told the flight attendant about the special passengers with us, and she consulted with the captain. He promptly moved them all to first class. At the end of the flight he announced, "We have some special passengers on board with us today, coming home from Iraq. Can you show them how happy you are to have them on board with you?" The plane erupted with shouts and cheers and applause. I have to admit that I teared right up, full of gratitude not only for those ten brave young men and women, but also for the flight attendant, the captain, and the cheering passengers who did such a heartwarming job of showing their appreciation.

Every summer midshipmen fan out across the country to do summer trainings. Some of them end up in Alaska for the National Outdoor Leadership School (NOLS) trainings. And every summer without fail, one couple—the parents of three USNA graduates—picks up dozens of midshipmen at the airport, then houses them, feeds them, and transports them to the course site, all without any kind of compensation. "My husband and I host mids because we love your Navy sons and daughters as if they were our own," this lifelong Alaskan mom wants USNA parents to know. "And we know that wherever our children go, there will be other Navy parents to watch out for them." It's exceptionally generous—and it's what military families do for each other.

I have lived in a small farming town for the last twenty-seven years. People there really know how to come together and support one another in a time of need. But after growing up as a military kid, and now, being a military mom, I will say that the military community is unmatched when it comes to meeting needs at warp speed. My friend Denise knows this, too. "My daughter was on a much-needed vacation in Rome when her wallet was stolen," she told me. "She was stranded without money or identification. I immediately put out an online SOS, and a wonderful military wife who was living there helped her to replace her documents and get her funds right away. What a relief!"

Frequently an emergency call for assistance involves cars or weather. "My son or daughter has broken down on Highway XYZ," for instance. "Can anybody help?" And amazingly, within minutes it seems, military dads or moms show up bringing toolkits, jumper cables, and snacks—and most importantly, peace of mind for the mom on the other end of the line. Your son or daughter is stranded at an airport because of weather? People will hop into their four-wheel drive vehicles to brave the elements and pick up your child so he or she doesn't spend the night in the airport.

Occasionally, though, a blizzard or flood might get in the way of the military emergency rescue squad. Once, Brendan was traveling back to college and was stuck overnight in the Minneapolis-St. Paul airport during a blizzard. Somehow during a long night on uncomfortable airport chairs, his military ID slipped out of his pocket. What a hassle to replace it, not to mention the fact that it's a security risk for a military ID to be floating around. He was still beating himself up about it a few days later when we received a phone call from a gentleman who had found the ID and tracked him down. Later, a package arrived with the ID and a note.

Brendan,

Keep yourself safe in theater. Take care of your men and they will take care of you.

Thank you for your service. We are a grateful nation.

Sincerely,
Bob XXX-USN Retired

When I think of Bob and all those people young and old who step forward to support and honor our troops in any way they can, I realize once again, for the thousandth time, or maybe the millionth, that no military parent needs to be alone with his or her worries and fears. There are countless Americans, individually or as part of parent groups or other organizations, who are reaching out to our servicemen and women to say thank you to or send cookies or phone cards or knit helmet liners and warm scarves. When I am missing my kids or am worried about them, it helps me to remember that I am part of a huge extended family that is there for my children and me. And that there are others who aren't even a part of the family who offer kindnesses that I will probably never even know about. I could never have imagined the extent to which this is true before my kids joined the military and they, and I, began to experience it firsthand.

And you, too, dear fellow military mom, are a part of the biggest family in the world—that sprawling, sometimes unruly, but exceedingly loyal, military family. And you, too, will have the opportunity to do unto another mom's child what you would have done unto your own, whether it's with a simple "thank you" at the mall, a pot of homemade chicken noodle soup delivered to a sick cadet, or an offer to house a soldier stranded overnight in an unfamiliar city due to a flight delay. So let me offer you right now my most heartfelt and sincere thanks—for the service of your children, and for your own generosity and service, too. Bravo Zulu to you all!

Love in the Mail

I t's care package day at Brye Farm. The table is covered with flat-rate boxes from the post office, and the aromas of the all-day baking extravaganza still linger in the air—after all, what's a package from home without some homemade goodies? Organized nearby in assembly-line fashion are Oreos, ChapSticks, baby wipes, lemon drops, books of word games and Sudoku puzzles, photos, and packages of toothpaste and sunscreen and body lotion. There are random silly toys from the dollar store that I have collected over the weeks, and local newspapers, and magazines: *Runner's World, ESPN, National Geographic,* and *Time.* I start loading up the boxes—four for my own kids plus some extras for those who might need a boost.

The whole uncut pan of brownies, sealed in a Ziploc bag and wrapped in foil, goes into Eric's box. I tuck the chocolate chip cookies in the Pringles cans—it would not be a care package for Brendan without his childhood favorites. The lemon drop candies and ChapStick are for Jordan, who always seems to be fighting a cold when he's deployed. Of course, he has to have a few Pringles cans full of chocolate chip cookies—they're his favorites, too—and the pie-in-the-canning-jar also goes in his box. Sudoku books and girlie body lotion are for Katrina, who will smile when she sees them and then dive into the latest issue of *Runner's World*. I fill boxes for other mothers' children, mothers who perhaps cannot send care packages right now. I send silly cards, Christmas decorations, Halloween candy—anything that might break the monotony or disrupt the loneliness of being far from home. I imagine my kids and the other recipients ripping open the packages and laughing as they see the fake mustaches, the goofy candy teeth, and the Tootsie Pops.

To many families these funny, mundane treats are just items on a shopping list, items that you toss in your cart as you wander through a giant grocery store. Oreos are just an after school snack. Toothpaste is just a basic toiletry. Who cares if you run out of ChapStick? You can always pick up some more tomorrow. But to my family and military families across the country, Oreos are not just Oreos. Oreos are *home*, especially when combined with milk. Toothpaste means "Don't forget to brush, honey." Lemon drops and ChapStick mean "I'm sorry you don't feel well." Magazines are a distraction from the monotony of life in a war zone or on a ship far from home. And scented body lotion? That means "I know you're still a girl underneath all that body armor." In other words, all these goodies from home are more than just goodies. They say "I know you miss the tastes, smells, and pleasures of home." They say "I'm thinking of you, sweetie." They say "Take care of yourself and be safe." They say "Here's some love in the mail."

Those of us who have been military moms for a while know that there are many troops who have few resources and little or no family support. This is one of the reasons that so many moms stand on their heads to get care packages out to their kids when they're forward deployed; those care packages aren't just for their own children, they are for those young men and women who get no mail, no packages, and who would be essentially alone without their military family. I know lots of parents who have "adopted" someone at the request of a son or daughter. We are a family linked by duty, honor, and service.

That family has stepped up time and time again to provide for each other's offspring. One of my favorite stories of care package support involves Santa and his elves—sort of. Back in 2012, I knew that many of Eric's Marines had no family backing. And as fortune (or lack of fortune) would have it, the company was deployed for both Thanksgiving and Christmas two years in a row. When word came of that second consecutive year of holiday deployment, I decided I wanted to send some supplementary cheer to the company. With Eric's permission, I sent out an e-mail to my parent friends, hopeful that we could collect at least enough to offer something to those in most need. Then I waited to hear from Eric regarding the results. Sometime thereafter he was gone on a mission for a few days, and when he returned, the sergeant major tracked him down. "Who *are* you, Captain Brye? Santa Claus? There are so many packages in the mail room the clerks can't move!"

No, Sergeant Major, Eric isn't Santa Claus, but the Sisterhood of military moms (and honorary dads) makes a fine band of elves. It was a sweeter holiday for lots of those Marines, and for all of us at home, as well.

June, the Marine mother who adopted me when I was a brand new military mom, found a great use for some of the small toys left over from a Christmas party that she and a group of Girl Scout troops and their parents had put on for military children and their parents. She filled a box full of yo-yos, penlight pointers, squishy balls that lit up, and the like, and sent it to her son, who was working overseas in a secure area in a highly stressful environment. I don't know about you, but my experience with boys—young ones, at least—is that they will automatically kick, throw, or bounce any spherical object within reach. Sure enough, her son reported that when he opened the box and distributed the yo-yos and other toys, it brought out the kid in everyone, and they were able to laugh together and enjoy some desperately needed relief from the tension of their long workdays. I love the thought of these highly trained and consummately fit young men releasing their stress by engaging in yo-yo competitions and pelting each other with light-up squishy balls.

Some time ago I heard of a group of women who meet monthly to box up the pounds and pounds of cookies, often well over two hundred pounds, that they and other volunteers bake to send to deployed military personnel. The organization—SOS Cookies, which stands for Send Our Soldiers Cookies—started in 2007 when one Florida grandmother was looking for something to do for her grandson, who was deployed in Iraq. Eight years later, anywhere from twelve to twenty women, many in their eighties, show up every month, and they send tens of thousands of cookies overseas yearly. "At Christmas, it's standing room only when we meet to pack the boxes," Rita, the group's founder, reports, "and we've been known to send as many as four hundred pounds of cookies in our holiday shipment alone!"

Perhaps my favorite care package story of all involves a fellow Marine mom who had written to me prior to one holiday season when Eric was deployed, asking if she could add his name to her local civic organization's care package list. I said sure, but that he also had some men in his unit who would appreciate packages, too.

"How many?" she wrote back.

"Well, there are two hundred and twenty-five in his unit," I responded, "but any little bit helps." I was stunned when she said that they would take care of the entire unit! Two hundred and twenty-five care packages! Wow! And just as amazing, when it came time for these young men and women to return to the States, the organization sponsored welcome home care packages that included toiletries and gift cards for every single one of them! Two hundred and twenty-five *more* care packages! I believe that kind of love in action is good for more than just the body; I believe it's good for the soul of every single person on both the giving and the receiving end of it.

When my kids first entered the military, care packages were a fun way to send them love from home, and sending them gave me something real and tangible to do, providing an outlet for my anxiety and worry. But I didn't *really* comprehend just how vital care packages are to our soldiers—how much impact they have—until a letter came from Bill, a Marine major I've known since he was a baby.

Bill is the oldest son of my long-time friend and fellow military mom, Frances. Bill eventually became a Marine officer and was sent to Iraq, where he and his men faced a particularly tough situation. I promptly asked the USNA-Parents listserv to send care packages to me so that I could send them on to him and his troops. I never did that again. Why? Because before I knew it, I had packages stacked floor to ceiling across my living room! I wised up fast and asked that any additional packages be sent directly to the unit. Ultimately his company, plus two more companies, benefited from the outpouring of generosity. Later in the year, I received this note from Bill, which I forwarded on to those who had sent packages:

Family & Friends,

I am headed out to Iraq again today and wanted to send an e-mail to everyone that has written, sent packages, or simply said thank you. This past year has been an amazing chance to do amazing things. To meet new people, and truly appreciate how lucky we are to live in this country, no matter how many faults it has. For those of you who don't know, I was scheduled to ship out to Okinawa but the day before my unit left I was transferred to a unit going back to Iraq. (For the sake of my parents' sanity, I was "voluntold" to do it and that's my story and I am sticking to it.) Whatever the truth may be, my place is back in Iraq with all my brothers in harm's way.

We will see this thing through to the end. A little bit of encouragement is always appreciated, so please drop me an e-mail anytime and let me know how life is going back in the States.

I was happy to hear that all those letters, e-mails, and packages had really made a difference to him and his men, and knowing Bill I was sure that "a little bit of encouragement is always appreciated" was something of an understatement.

The letter continued:

The author of my favorite novel and a very wise man once wrote, "All my life one question has haunted me. What is the opposite of fear? To call it aphobia, fearlessness, is without meaning. This is just a name, thesis expressed as antithesis. . . . I want to *know the true obverse, as day of night and heaven of earth . . . [for] is not acting out of fear of dishonor still, in essence, acting out of fear? The opposite of fear must be something nobler. A higher form of the mystery. Pure, infallible. . . . The opposite of fear is love."**

As I read the letter, tears filled my eyes, and I found myself wanting to cry. The fact that this young man was contemplating such heady thoughts as he prepared to put himself in harm's way reminded me yet again—as if I ever need reminding—that so many of our country's best and brightest are indeed wearing military uniforms.

If the opposite of fear is indeed love, then maybe love can act as an antidote to fear. And if love can act as an antidote to fear, I propose that we all remember to keep sending love in the mail—lots and lots of love in the mail.

---

* Steven Pressfield, *The Gates of Fire* (New York: Doubleday, 1998).

It's Okay If You Break Down
in the Dairy Aisle

*C*artons of eggs. Quarts of milk. Packages of thin-sliced ched-
dar cheese. In an instant, these items go blurry as tears well
in my eyes, and the next thing I know I'm overtaken by sobs. My
old friend Trisha, who I've just run into in the local grocery store,
stares wide-eyed and rubs my back delicately, like she might break
me. Moments ago, I'd happily encountered Trisha, a mom of one
of Katrina's high school classmates, who I hadn't seen in ages. She
gave me a rundown on her new grandchild and the goings-on of her
family members, all of whom live within two miles of her, and then
casually asked about mine. I opened my mouth to answer, but no
words came out. What could I say to her about my kids? That they
were scattered all over the country? That Eric was deploying for the
second time in two years? That Jordan had just left his five-month-
old daughter and was flying in a place that had me scared spitless?
Usually, I'm able to eke out a pat answer to the casual questions
about my children and their whereabouts. "They're good, I'm fine.

Getting by." But for some reason on this particular morning, I lost it. For most people, the fluorescent-lit dairy aisle of their local Giant Eagle hardly invites an emotional breakdown, but if I've learned one thing in the last decade and a half of being a military mom, it's that the freight train of emotions can come thundering around the corner at any moment and overtake you when you least expect it. And so there I stood, shoulders heaving and blubbering, next to the neatly stacked cartons of whipped butter and cottage cheese.

Offer it up. That's what my mom and the nuns at Catholic school advised when my brothers, sisters, and classmates voiced any complaint, whether it was pedestrian childish whining or the result of a true ailment. We were supposed to *offer up* our anxieties, worries, fears, frustrations, and physical pains to God, and then take comfort in the knowledge that we would no longer have to deal with them ourselves because He had it covered. In other words, we were supposed to get over it. And growing up in the quintessentially military family that I did, surrounded by other military families, the prevailing ethos was to "suck it up" or "embrace the suck."

Offer it up. Get over it. Suck it up. Embrace the suck.

Okay. Sure. I can do all of that. I wholeheartedly support all of my children and all who are serving, and I will do whatever it takes to stand behind them. Our military children need us to be strong back home while they are on the front lines. I can embrace the suck, and so can every other military mother I know. But sometimes being the wind beneath our kids' wings is exhausting. Sometimes I just want to say, to myself or to anyone who will listen, "This is really, really hard." Usually, I don't.

There have been plenty of times when neighbors or nonmilitary friends or acquaintances ask me how I'm doing and—I'm not going to lie here—I can see that they don't really want to know, that they're just making small talk. I'm not being critical here. That's what most of us have been raised to do, right? Make polite small talk. So I just say, "Oh, you know, okay. Getting by." Or maybe they do really want to know, and I can see that, too, but my answer is still the same. Usually that's because I'm feeling vulnerable, and I'm afraid that if I start crying, I won't be able to stop. That's fine. I reserve the right to protect myself when I'm feeling really raw. Very occasionally I will tell the truth to a nonmilitary friend when I can see that she is asking because she really wants to know and is willing to listen to the truth. Very, very occasionally.

Here's the truth. When my children are deployed, I begin standing watch. It's exhausting duty. It continues day after day, night after night. It's as if I'm a sentry who never gets relieved, or I'm patrolling the perimeter, isolated from all that's normal in my life. In fact, it's almost like I'm on my own deployment. To try to explain the experience of this hypervigilant paradigm to someone who has not ever been or will not ever be in this position takes too much effort.

When people ask, for instance, "Where is he?" and I reply "Asia," and then they say smile and say, as if everything is just hunky dory, "Oh, aren't you glad it isn't Afghanistan?"

"No!" I want to scream. "Haven't you heard about the P-3 forced down by the Chinese Air Force? Or the aircraft accidents? Or how about the North Koreans and their antiaircraft missiles?"

But I realize I might sound like a crazy person, so I bite my lip—my stiff upper lip—and retreat back to the isolated world where other military moms and I measure time by the number of days until their kids return to CONUS. If I stop long enough to tell you what it's really like and how I really feel, well, I just might fall apart. And I really don't want to fall apart. Sentries must stay alert at all times.

Or so I've felt until recently. Lately I've been wondering if maybe I need to make the effort to be a little more real in response to the small talk and the well-intentioned remarks. For one thing, if I maintain a stiff upper lip too long, my facial muscles begin to cramp. So maybe it's actually a positive thing for me to relax that stiff upper lip so that people can see how hard life with loved ones in the military is on me. On you. On all military family members. If we are going to get the support we need, we need to be honest about the costs to us.

So from now on, I don't want to pretend when nonmilitary friends and acquaintances ask me how I'm doing. And I don't want them to "protect" me, either.

I live on the edge of the Appalachians in Ohio farm country. There are a few other military families in our area, but not that many. As my kids moved toward and into lives at the Naval Academy and beyond, I found myself feeling increasingly isolated and unable to connect with neighboring parents. Don't get me wrong. I appreciate them. We sat side by side on bleachers together for years, and baked for bake sales and volunteered and celebrated elementary school and middle school and high school graduations together. But as they prepared to send their kids to college, I prepared to send mine to a place where I had far more to worry about than the freshman fifteen.

At that moment when your child's path diverges so dramatically from the paths of his or her friends, a fault line between you and those friends' mothers can appear. Sometimes that fault line is tiny, just a hairline fracture, and you and your fellow soccer moms and PTA buddies can remain as bonded as you ever were. In my experience, though, that fault line can expand into a great chasm dividing military moms and nonmilitary moms. Suddenly all that time spent sharing bleachers and car pools doesn't quite bridge the gap between the incredibly different parenting challenges you each face now. And then when your kids start to deploy—well, the chasm can become so wide it's almost like you're living on different planets. In the beginning people would ask me how my kids were, but if my nerves had the best of me that day I would tell them how frightened I was and begin to cry. There's nothing like breaking down in the dairy aisle—or the hardware store or the post office—to make you feel exposed and ridiculous.

I know all those people who prompted a momentary display of weepiness from me were sad to upset me, and many of them stopped asking about my kids. I know they still care; it's just that they're uncomfortable with strong emotions, or they don't want to cause me pain. "No one understands what you're going through unless they have gone through it themselves," one Marine mom told me. "'We will be praying for him,' they all say. But nobody asks me how I *feel*. They don't want to know. It's just too uncomfortable for them." Another Army mom told me that when her son deployed, people responded almost as if he had died. No one wanted her to cry or get upset, so they just stayed away. No news is good news, right?

Ouch.

Upset her? Upset me? Upset any of the military parents who have children deployed in a war zone? Nothing anyone could do or say could possibly be any worse than the stress of worrying about a kid at war. The result of not being asked, with genuine concern, how I'm doing—and of my not answering honestly—is increased isolation. It leads to my feeling that I need to cultivate a strong and calm and in-control persona, even in those moments when I don't feel it. Yes, I am often strong and calm and in control. I've had plenty of time to work at it. But trust me, I am not strong and calm and in control all the time, not even close. Ask my husband and my kids.

If I were strong and calm and in control all the time, I wouldn't be human—or at least I wouldn't be a mother.

In a strange way, not being asked how I'm doing, or how my kids are doing, reminds me of an observation that I've heard voiced by people with cancer or other serious illnesses. The more challenging an illness is and the graver the prognosis, the more uncomfortable many people seem to get around the ill person. The bigger the worries we have, the easier it is to stay away from us. But it's when we have big worries that we need people around more than ever.

I got a touching lesson in what I needed as a military mom from the nonmilitary community from a surprising place: a classroom full of usually disengaged high school juniors. It was Veterans Day, and just before our school's celebratory assembly started, I had gotten word that a good friend's son was seriously injured by an IED; his mother had been told that his odds of survival were about 4 percent. I spent most of the assembly in the school's darkened auditorium wiping away the tears streaming down my face. When the assembly finally ended, I made a fairly successful effort to compose myself. After all, I had the water cycle to teach.

A few minutes after class started, I was drawing a diagram on the blackboard when I was overtaken by sobs. I don't mean that gentle little tears started to escape from my eyes, I mean I was completely overtaken by wracking sobs, as in literally unable to function. I managed to gulp out "Not my kid" so the students would know that my children were okay. And then, in an instant it seemed, lots and lots of loving arms surrounded me. These "problem" kids, who on any other day would sit practically catatonic, uninterested in the greater world beyond them, were comforting me and bringing me back from the edge of despair.

Those hugs meant the world to me that day. They mean the world to me any day. As strong as I am, I just don't have it in me to be brave every hour of every day. And in those moments when I don't, knowing that I can be honest and let go lightens the burden I carry. And if you're not part of a military family and you don't know how to relate to this display of emotion—well, you don't have to do a thing but listen and try to understand. That's all I need. Really.

When you don't, it's hard for those of us who *are* part of a military family not to feel isolated sometimes, as plenty of military moms out there will attest to. "Some days I want someone to stop and really look me in the eyes when they ask how my daughter is doing on her deployment. I want to know that I don't have to censor it to protect them," Air Force mom Lisa writes. "I want to say I am worried that the things she is seeing and experiencing may change her forever. But instead I hold back, because that is not normal chatter in the teachers' lounge. It's just so foreign to everyone else's worries that I might as well be talking about what to pack for a trip to the moon."

And if Lisa and I feel isolated from time to time, consider the Special Forces mom who mused, "How do I respond to someone who asks me what my son does when I know he's a trained killer who steps into harm's way regularly? It's not easy to strike up a conversation about that. Of course, I couldn't say anything even if I wanted to. I need to maintain silence about that in order to keep my son and his family safe. So when new acquaintances ask me what he does, I just say 'Security.'

"Other longtime friends and acquaintances who have a sense of what he does simply don't ask about him. It makes them too uncomfortable, almost as if he had a terrible disease. Still others tell me, 'I would never let *my* son do something like that.' Is that supposed to be comforting? As if I had any control over it!"

My friend Melissa comes from four generations of pacifists. They don't know what to think or say about the warrior that emerged from their peace-loving family. But it's almost as if he had been called. "There is organized evil in the world, and someone has to do something about it," he told his mother. He has chosen to be one of those people who does something about it.

How does this mom cope? "I look for comfort in doing things for others. I knit and make American hero quilts with a quilting group. I garden. I babysit for foster parents. Busy hands divert the mind from the heart. I do know that I have less patience with trivial things and drama, and I avoid stress. I have enough drama and stress already. And I cultivate a few military parent friends who I can communicate with. I don't know the details of my son's life, but I know enough that my heart cries, and they can understand."

We all feel our hearts crying sometimes, even if we don't show it. That's why we need people. We need people to talk to, and people to wrap their arms around us, both literally and figuratively. The most helpful people in our lives are those who get it, and we gravitate toward them. We all need to talk to or cry with or sometimes just sit silently with someone who understands. And if someone who cares about us doesn't understand, well, he or she can be trained.

So please remember that those who are not in the military can be important parts of our support systems, too. And when it comes to getting the sort of support you need from them, remember that honesty is the best policy. Most people are not mind readers, and it really helps them if you tell them what kind of support you'd like.

With that said, I'm going to take a moment to practice what I preach by reaching out to any civilian readers right now. I hope my doing so will make it easier for you, fellow military mom, to ask for whatever support you'd like from the nonmilitary people in your life, too.

If you're a civilian friend or acquaintance—or maybe even a stranger, or someone who I've just met—and you see me in the post office or the airport or the classroom or the dairy aisle—and know that when I say "me" I mean the collective community of military moms and dads—don't just thank me for my children's service, ask me how they are doing. Ask me how I am doing. And if I start to cry, hug me. Hug me hard. If you can't do that, squeeze my hand. Tell me you will be thinking about my kids and me every day. Send me a card just because. Send my kid a care package. Send his or her spouse or kids a care package. Send me a care package! (Just kidding.) Show me you have not forgotten my loved ones. And when bad news is in the newspapers or online or on the television, call me and tell me that you're thinking of me. Don't be afraid of my tears, or anger, or other strong emotions. It's okay for me to get upset, I can handle it. And so can you. It's good that we want to protect each other, but sometimes it's better to talk. Or to hug. Or to do anything but ignore the truth of the situation. We need to be honest with each other because ultimately, military and nonmilitary families alike, we are all in this together. Our military kids are our future, and our collective freedom depends on them.

Support from
Unexpected Places

1 held the invitation in my hand and stared at it in disbelief.

THE PRESIDENT AND MRS. OBAMA
REQUEST THE PLEASURE OF THE COMPANY OF
MRS. ELAINE BRYE AND GUEST
AT A DINNER IN HONOR OF
THE RIGHT HONOURABLE
DAVID CAMERON, M.P.
PRIME MINISTER OF THE UNITED KINGDOM AND
NORTHERN IRELAND
and
MRS. SAMANTHA CAMERON

My first thought, when I had a coherent thought again, was that this must be some sort of joke. But it would have had to be an expensive joke, given the weight of the paper and all that elegant calligraphy.

I was at a complete loss as to why I'd been invited to a state dinner at the White House. I wasn't active politically, and in fact,

I wasn't even a Democrat. Then I remembered the Christmas card I'd sent three months earlier, in December. When my first grandchild was five months old, her father, Jordan, was deployed for seven months. My heart was heavy at the thought of all the precious milestones he would miss and the fact that she might not even recognize him when he returned. I wondered what kind of supports would be available for my daughter-in-law, Angela, and their sweet baby girl, and so, in my typical Type A fashion, I began to investigate.

I had been vaguely aware that First Lady Michelle Obama and Dr. Jill Biden had been doing military outreach, but I'd had no idea that they were spending so much time traveling to military bases and visiting with families, or that they'd created an initiative, called Joining Forces, to support the military and their families. When I saw the words *When our troops serve, their families are serving, too* on the Joining Forces page of the White House website, I felt a combination of happiness and relief and gratitude wash over me. *Somebody understands!* I thought. *And it's somebody who's doing something about it!*

So when it came time to send out Christmas cards later that year, I decided to send a card to the first lady to thank her for her work on behalf of military families. Proud mom that I am, of course I told her about my four children and their military service. I mailed the card, which featured a photograph of all four kids in uniform, and then focused on the holidays, the new grandchild that was due soon, and Jordan's approaching homecoming. Then, in February, I flew to Bangladesh to visit Courtney, who was training commercial pilots there.

When I arrived home a month later, there was a cream-colored envelope with beautiful flowing script buried in all the mail that had accumulated during my absence. Was it really possible that someone at the White House read all of the Christmas cards the president and the first lady received? And that as a result of my card I was now being invited to a state dinner? Which was to occur the following week?! As strange as that seemed to me, it was the only thing I could figure out. I called Courtney in Bangladesh and woke him up—it was the middle of the night there—and told him I thought he better start making plans to get home. I think he thought I was jet-lagged out of my mind.

The next day I called the White House Social Office and found out that sure enough, the invitation was real. I accelerated into planning and logistics mode, and, more importantly, started dress shopping. A former Naval Academy commandant had nicknamed me the Purple Mom, because purple is the color of the joint forces and I have a child in four of the five branches. I found a purple gown and added my four rhinestone service pins, one in honor of each service branch represented in our family—and in honor of each of my children, who are my most precious gems of all. And after a week of hustling and bustling, Courtney and I found ourselves standing at the special visitor's entrance to the White House, feeling a little bit like Ma and Pa Kettle.

With all my nervousness about meeting the president and first lady, and my worries about what to wear, I had never thought about all the other important people who would be there. In fact, the guest list included 360 dignitaries from the United States and the United Kingdom, and as I looked around the room I wondered who in the world we would talk to. I clung to Courtney's hand and said a prayer.

I needn't have worried. Everyone was so friendly, especially when they found out about our four military kids. In one of the first hospitality rooms we entered, I saw General John Allen, resplendent in his mess dress; he'd been the Commandant of Midshipmen at the Naval Academy when Eric and Jordan had been there. I hadn't really known him personally but still, he felt like a safe haven, and

Courtney and I had a warm conversation with him and his wife. As we moved on upstairs, I told Courtney that my night was complete; I couldn't imagine anything more exciting than that.

But there was more to come. We were impressed by the respect shown again and again for our children's service. Most of the military aides knew at least one of our children from either the Naval Academy or from Jordan's exchange semester at the Coast Guard Academy. We were absolutely thrilled when we were escorted across the room to meet one of our nation's newest Medal of Honor recipients, Sergeant First Class Leroy Petry, and his wife. What a privilege.

Finally it was time to go through the receiving line to meet the president and first lady and Prime Minister Cameron and his wife. After being greeted warmly by the two heads of state, I was greeted by Mrs. Obama. We chatted for a brief moment, and then she said, "We'll have plenty of time to continue talking later. You're sitting at our table." And then she enveloped me in a huge hug.

I was flabbergasted. If I had tried to dream up a more unlikely and thrilling scenario even in my wildest of fantasies, I couldn't have. The first thing I did was run to the ladies room, where I made a surreptitious call to my daughter to share the news. I'm pretty sure she thought all the excitement had made me delirious.

I was seated diagonally across from the first lady and George Clooney. Courtney sat across from Prime Minister Cameron and SFC Petry and Damien Lewis from the Showtime series *Homeland*. Warren Buffett was at the table along with his daughter Susie, who was on my right. To say the least, it was a very congenial and interesting group. Mrs. Obama and I talked about parenting, like moms do when they get together, and she asked why I thought all of ours had chosen to serve. She talked about the need to do more for the families of those in service. When I told her how Courtney, a Vietnam veteran with three Air Medals, was treated when he returned from that war, and how I had been spit at while attending college classes in my ROTC uniform so many years ago, she said, "Never again."

After the sumptuous meal, the evening continued with great music and friendly conversation. I'd found myself exchanging small talk with George Clooney during dinner. Later, when it came out that I'd taught in Afghanistan for a year, we had a deeper conversation about how to make a difference in developing countries. Over and over again throughout the evening, people, including the president, thanked us for our children's service. When it was all over, Courtney and I agreed it was the experience of a lifetime. I was feeling a little like Cinderella after the ball as we headed back to the farm.

Life moved on. Five months later, in August, we were at a gas station in South Dakota on the way home from a visit to my mother-in-law when my cell phone rang. "Hi Elaine. It's Olivia, Michelle Obama's press secretary," a friendly voice said. "The first lady is wondering if you would be her guest at the Democratic National Convention next month in Charlotte, North Carolina."

I think I asked Olivia to repeat herself. Or maybe I just said, "Huh?" Then Olivia continued. "And would you be willing to speak for five minutes about the needs of military families?"

I hesitated. I wasn't afraid to speak. I expected that the five minutes would most likely come during one of the untelevised filler time slots, and that all the delegates would be milling about on the floor of the convention center, and that it would be noisy, and no one would be listening to what I had to say. My hesitation came from my concern about any repercussions on my children. Also, I have always been very private about my political beliefs. That goes back to the way I was raised growing up in the military.

I told Olivia that I would have to get back to her.

Stunned, Courtney and I decided to tell no one about the invitation except our children, who would need to run the development by their Public Affairs officers. After it was clear that my participation would not affect them, I agreed to attend and to speak.

Several days later, we were parked in our camper in Hannibal, Missouri, waiting out a rainstorm that had interrupted our journey home. My phone rang, and to my shock it was once again the White House. "Elaine, I hate to bother you," Olivia said, "but we have one more question. The first lady would be honored if you would introduce her at the convention. She is so touched by your family's service that she wants to share your story with America. Would you be willing?"

I was speechless. The White House knew that Courtney and I were Republicans, and that we hadn't made a choice yet about how we were going to vote. Eventually I must have said something to Olivia, but I'm not sure what; it takes a lot to make me speechless. I do know that I didn't make a decision on the spot.

Courtney and I prayed and discussed it, and I reached a real peace about making the appearance. I knew there would be those who would not understand my choice, but I felt strongly that bringing greater public awareness to the ongoing need for support for military members and their families was a goal I wanted to serve. I'd been supporting military families at the Naval Academy for years. This, I told myself, was just a way to do it on a larger scale. And so a few weeks later I found myself ready to walk out on a stage before thousands of convention delegates and a television audience of millions. As I waited, I thought about my parents and their service, and about my children. I thought about all the times Courtney and my dad and my kids had been in harm's way, and told myself that speaking at the convention was nothing compared to being shot at. I prayed that I would honor them and all who serve, and all my fellow military parents, as I shared a brief bit of my life as a military mom.

Finally, it was time, and I made that long walk to the podium that I had practiced. At the last minute, I had decided not to wear the heels my husband had carried around all day. I just didn't want to slip and fall, so I wore my lucky red flats, a purple dress, and my service pins.

As soon as I appeared onstage, the entire Ohio delegation rose to their feet and the audience cheered. When I spoke my first line— "What's a mom like me doing in a place like this?"—the audience roared with laughter. And then we were off. When the picture of my military kids was displayed behind me, the audience went wild. As I spoke of not knowing when I would be able to get all my children together again because someone was always deploying, my voice caught. But I held it together, and the next thing I knew, everyone was standing, and the first lady was meeting me onstage. "You were amazing," she said, giving me a hug. "I know I'll do fine now after that introduction."

After her speech and a flurry of interviews, Courtney and I finally headed back to our hotel, where I turned on my cell phone to find a string of text messages and e-mails. Most important, I had texts and voice messages from my family. Brendan, my Army son, may have left my favorite: "Good job, Mom," he said simply. Have I mentioned that all of my sons, like their father, are men of few words?

When I spoke to my mother the next day, she said, "You nailed it, Elaine. Good job. But you were wearing flats."

I had to laugh. "Yes ma'am, I was." Longtime military wife that she was, her sense of dress code had been just slightly offended. Remember that she came from the era of starching her uniform twice a day, and of white gloves and hats. All the same, there was plenty of pride in her voice.

Courtney and I stayed for the rest of the week, and it seemed like everywhere we went people thanked us for our children's service and told us they were praying for them. Never had I experienced such an outpouring of support for military families. I was moved, and heartened, and a little overwhelmed.

In the midst of all of the hubbub, we received an e-mail invitation to join the first lady in her box for former president Bill Clinton's speech, which we were honored to do. Vice President Biden's box was next to hers, and he was seated below me. During a break, I tapped his shoulder, because I wanted to meet his wife, Dr. Jill Biden, to thank her for cofounding the Joining Forces initiative with Mrs. Obama. When he felt my tap he turned around and beamed, saying, "You did a helluva job. Get down here!" He pulled me down the knee-high step, gave me a big hug, and then turned to his wife.

"Jillie, look who's here!"

Dr. Biden practically jumped into my arms and cried, telling me what an awesome speech I'd given. Not everyone knows that she is a military mom, too. She knows what it means to have a son at war.

The next moment can only be described as ludicrous. I needed to get back up to my seat, but it would be a breach of etiquette to cross in front of the first lady. It was twenty inches to the next row up, without a step. I knew I would have to find a way to scramble up somehow. I took a breath and raised one knee to try to make the step. Then suddenly the vice president was pushing me from behind, and another guest was pulling my arm from above. I think my husband was busy laughing, but I'm not sure because I was too busy praying that no cameras were trained on the box. God has a way of keeping us humble, even in our biggest moments.

What Holds Us Together

I Believe in Miracles

There I was, standing awkwardly with my breast smushed like a pancake between the cold glass plates. I was late—very late—getting my annual mammogram, due to one of my stubborn idiosyncrasies: If one of my kids is deployed I cannot possibly add one more stressful thing to my plate, and so I don't. A mammogram definitely fits in the category of stressful things on the plate. But my son Eric had just returned from seven months in an undisclosed location, and I needed to get it done. No more procrastinating.

Connie, the mammogram X-ray technician, had just one more view to take when she casually mentioned she had a son in the Army.

"Really? So do I," I responded, trying to keep my mind off my discomfort. Actually, the mention of her son *did* take my mind off my discomfort.

"Yes," she said, "and he's in Afghanistan. Now hold right there. Don't move. Don't breathe."

I stayed as motionless as possible until she told me I could exhale again.

"Afghanistan!" I said, feeling an immediate connection. "My son just came back from the Middle East. How do you cope?"

"Pray, pray, pray, pray, pray," she answered. "Every time I think about him or his wife and little boy I am just on my knees."

I asked her if she knew Psalm 91, The Warrior's Psalm, which promises the guardianship of angels, protection for the faithful from dangers seen and unseen, and the satisfaction of a long life. Whether Christian or Jewish, many of our warriors who put their faith in God—and many of those warriors' families—find comfort and encouragement in this outpouring of reassurance. Connie had never heard The Warrior's Psalm. And so that morning we sat down together in the X-ray room, me in my hospital gown and Connie in her lab coat, and we read it together.

When we concluded our impromptu prayer session, Connie wrapped me in a huge embrace and said she was going to memorize the psalm so she would have it with her whenever fear crept in. And as I left the medical facility that day, I felt lighter than air.

As the saying goes, *there are no atheists in a foxhole.* And I don't think there are many atheists who have kids in a foxhole, either. One of my good friends, Lurline, sums up this wisdom perfectly: "If you aren't a person of faith before your child enters the military, you really need to find a faith fast. You will be praying like nobody's business in times of trouble."

Praying like nobody's business—now there's an understatement if I've ever heard one. I have the Lord on speed dial. Just like Connie, my X-ray technician, I "pray, pray, pray, pray, pray." I pray for good leadership, for airplanes not falling out of the sky, for protection from enemies seen and unseen. I pray when I knit. I pray when I'm in church. When driving. When washing dishes. I pray as I drift off to sleep at night and sometimes before I open my eyes in the morning. And yes, I even pray for my kids when I'm half-dressed in a hospital gown during a routine mammogram.

As I consider what sustains me in this crazy "Where's Waldo" roller coaster of a life that is part and parcel of having four kids in the military, I cannot begin to explain my survival without talking about faith. A deep, abiding faith is as woven into my family's DNA as military service is. My parents were devout Catholics, and not a week passed without every member of our family attending Mass at least once; my dad went to Mass every day that he could while he was deployed. As a child, I didn't understand why getting to church one or more times a week was such a big deal. Now I understand that the peace of the sanctuary and the familiarity of the service were anchors for both of my parents as we crisscrossed the country and globe during multiple moves and deployments. In my preteen years my biggest problem with religion was the bedlam that arose every Sunday morning as I tried to help my mom get seven kids dressed and ready for church.

"Where's the hairbrush, Elaine?"

"Look under your bed."

"Do I have to wear a slip?"

"Yes, Mary, you have to wear a slip . . . and underwear, too!"

During our first year in Virginia we went to Catholic school, where the nuns thought I had a calling to join them in the convent and devote my life to God. The reason? I was so intensely focused on reading about the lives of the saints. I didn't have the heart to tell them I was only reading about St. Francis and St. Michael and St. Joan because the tomes about them were the most exciting reading material in the library. But I did have a calling to try to make the world a better place. As I entered my teen years, I became very involved in the church youth groups wherever I was, and in doing good works in the community.

When I was sixteen, my dad went back to Vietnam. As I coped with my fears and struggled with the possibilities of what might happen to him, I started praying more often. Prayer became something I did not just in church, but outside of church, too. *Dear Lord, I might be thinking as I folded the laundry or did my homework or brushed my sister's hair, please watch over the sick and the lonely and the hurting. Please watch over my family—yes, especially my family, and most especially my father and his men and my brother, who won't stop crying, and please keep the helicopters flying and please grant us peace on earth. Amen.*

It wasn't until I was in college that I started to have an understanding of a relationship with God beyond a gimme list. Over the next decade, I discovered that developing a faith is like building a muscle, and daily prayer is your training. You have to keep practicing, so that when game day arrives, you're primed and ready.

I've had many game days over the past few decades. The first major test to my then-fledgling faith came during a trip to Hawaii, when Eric was just a toddler and I was seven months pregnant with Jordan. One day the surf was up, so I stayed tucked up on the beach away from the water with the baby as Courtney and two of my sisters— one there to help me with my active young son, and one who was on her honeymoon and visiting for a day with her new husband— bodysurfed. We passed an idyllic morning on the island paradise, and then sometime later in the day, I saw it—a huge rogue wave heading for shore. I tried to shout and warn everyone, but the roar was too loud. I scooped up Eric and ran. My sisters dove down, but Courtney was lying on an air mattress, oblivious. I watched helplessly as he rose to the crest of the monster wave and then disappeared into the crashing surf. When he reappeared, my stoic husband was screaming in pain, having been driven into the shore headfirst. "I broke my neck," he gasped when he could finally speak. After two weeks of misdiagnosis, further testing revealed that he was right.

Courtney had a fracture of the C-5 vertebra, resulting in the paralysis of his left shoulder and upper arm. The injury was problematic on many levels, but for an airline pilot, the stakes were especially high; it would mean the end of a career. If Courtney couldn't reach the switches on the cockpit panels, he couldn't fly. We ended up in the office of Dr. Joseph Maroon, a renowned neurosurgeon who was most fortunately based in Pittsburgh. He suggested what was at the time experimental surgery to replace the vertebra. There were no guarantees Courtney would ever be able to raise his arm again. In fact, it was possible that the surgery might result in complete paralysis from the neck down. But we felt we had no choice, so on a June morning in 1984 my husband underwent surgery in Allegheny General Hospital. I sat in the waiting room, seven months pregnant with an eighteen-month-old toddler at home, praying and wondering how I would cope with the outcome.

The surgeon came out with a smile that could have lit up a moonless night. "It's a miracle," he said. "We have never seen neck trauma like this that hasn't resulted in the patient becoming a paraplegic. We just asked your husband to raise his arm, and he raised it above his head. He is our miracle patient."

Throughout Courtney's recovery, two things remained constant: a steady stream of diapers, and scouting trips to find the farm of our dreams. After convincing my husband that despite the gift of two sons I really wanted to try for a girl, I was pregnant again in the spring of 1985. Two weeks after our baby girl arrived, I found our farm in Northeast Ohio. It seemed like the perfect place to raise our young children, and so we moved when Katrina was five months old. Life was a blur of chores and gardens and trying to fix up the old farmhouse. Courtney was flying on top of all this, of course, and so several years later when he complained of blood in his urine during hay-baling season, I chalked it up to dehydration exacerbated somehow by exhaustion. Nothing to worry about.

But his symptoms persisted and intensified, and I began to get scared. I finally wrangled him to a doctor and then to a specialist. When I saw the look on the doctor's face, I knew something was very wrong.

"I'm sorry to tell you that I think you have an extremely bad form of bladder cancer," he said to Courtney. "It's possible that you have less than two years to live. And by the way, how many children do you have?"

When I replied "three," speaking for the speechless Courtney, he turned to me and said, "That's good, because you won't be able to have any more if he survives." *If he survives*? We had three children under the age of six, plus animals and a farm to take care of. He couldn't die.

The only thing I could do was pray. The Psalms, those anguished cries for help, those prayers for God's protection, comforted me as we walked through the surgery and the endless period of waiting for biopsy results and treatment plans. And then, after three weeks, we had the answer—a rare benign tumor.

Another miracle!

And we were in for yet *another* miracle: exactly twelve months after the initial diagnosis, we welcomed a new baby boy into our lives—Brendan Phillip Brye, a spectacular testimony to God's loving care and provision.

When people ask me how I cope with fear as a military mother, I think of all the times I have been blessed when

I walked though dark valleys but was not alone. I count them as preparation for the times when my children are in harm's way.

So yes, I believe in miracles.

I also believe in guardian angels. At times when my heart is troubled, it's the image from Psalm 91—of angels watching over my children—that I cling to. And the thought that those blessed guardian angels are covering my children with their holy wings always gives me peace.

I've been relying on those heavenly protectors ever since the children were little. I could usually keep the kids safe with constant vigilance, but every once in a while my attention strayed for just a moment. One time when I was doing dishes, I suddenly heard an audible voice whisper in my ear: *Where's Eric?*

I stopped what I was doing and searched for the missing four-year-old, and after a couple of minutes I became somewhat frantic. There are just too many places on a farm that are dangerous for a little one. That includes our pond, which we cannot see from the house. We had a strictly enforced rule to never *ever* go to the pond without mom or dad. And then there was the voice again. *The pond.*

I rushed outside, and there he was, completely out of sight from the house and halfway down the lane to the pond, with a fishing pole on his shoulder.

A year later I had a similar experience. This time the voice said: *Where are the boys?*

I rushed out the back door and began yelling for them. After a moment, Jordan, age three, came out of the barn with a sheepish look on his face.

"Where's Eric?"

"Barn."

"You know you aren't allowed in the barn! Go to your room, Jordan. And Eric, get out here right now!"

As Jordan turned to go into the house and Eric emerged from the barn, I heard another prompt.

Ask them what they were doing.

I did, and Jordan looked up wide-eyed and said, "Fire!"

FIRE!!!! I ran into the barn and there it was on the floor of the hayloft, a campfire carefully constructed of loose hay and sticks that the boys had collected. Later the boys told me that it had caught several times, but blown out just as many—I can only imagine their guardian angels stomping it out—and now there was just a bit of smoke wafting into the rafters. It was a miracle that the entire barn had not gone ablaze, trapping them inside.

Today, I still count on my children's guardian angels to be on duty 24/7. Because of the nature of all of our children's deployments, we frequently don't know exactly where our kids are or when they're in more danger or less danger. The idea that their angels are on watch nonstop, even when I'm not sending prayers for extra protection their way, gives me peace. And I know that God's watchfulness extends to me and that no matter how bad things are or can seem, I am being cared for and protected.

So many of my fellow moms rely on prayer for comfort and strength. Maybe the prayers are offered during regular attendance at religious services, or maybe they are recited consistently morning and night, or maybe we take the shotgun approach to sending messages heavenward. It doesn't matter. For those of us who pray, the practice eases our minds, helps us deal with the loss of control we feel, and strengthens us.

My friend Jane shares, "Initially, after my son deployed, I felt so alone. And then I began praying every day without fail. And it helped so much. I expected his second deployment to be easier, but it wasn't. And then I realized I had gotten out of the habit of praying daily. When my husband and I started praying together again, I knew that God was there with us, listening. We had a friend who had been in Afghanistan who would stop in and pray with us. That was really powerful for some reason. The fact that he had been there."

Dana, a Navy mom, started attending Mass every day when her daughter left for boot camp. "Now, I continue that whether she's deployed or not. Her job is stressful no matter where she is—helping planes on a carrier is dangerous and accidents happen. I just want her to be covered in prayer all the time. Plus it makes me a better mom to start the day that way."

Yes, for so many of us in the Sisterhood, faith in a Higher Power is important. Essential, even. People often ask me what holds me together. They want to know where they can buy whatever magic glue, duct tape, or quadruple-ply yarn it is that keeps me from falling apart when I have two and sometimes three loved ones in harm's way. I can only point upward and answer "God's grace," and tell them they don't have to buy it, and better still, they can find it everywhere. For those of us who are people of faith, knowing that our children are part of God's divine plan confers a peace that holds us together even in the toughest times. And for that I am eternally grateful.

The Warrior's Psalm

1   *He who dwells in the shelter of the Most High*
      will rest in the shadow of the Almighty.

2   I will say of the Lord, "He is my refuge and my fortress,
my God, in whom I trust."
3   Surely he will save you from the fowler's snare
and from the deadly pestilence.
4   He will cover you with his feathers,
and under his wings you will find refuge;
his faithfulness will be your shield and rampart.
5   You will not fear the terror of night,
nor the arrow that flies by day,
6   nor the pestilence that stalks in the darkness,
nor the plague that destroys at midday.
7   A thousand may fall at your side,
ten thousand at your right hand,
but it will not come near you.
8   You will only observe with your eyes
and see the punishment of the wicked.
9   If you make the Most High your dwelling—
even the Lord, who is my refuge—
10   then no harm will befall you,
no disaster will come near your tent.
11   For he will command his angels concerning you
to guard you in all your ways;
12   they will lift you up in their hands,
so that you will not strike your foot against a stone.
13   You will tread upon the lion and the cobra;
you will trample the great lion and the serpent.
14   "Because he loves me," says the Lord, "I will rescue him;
I will protect him, for he acknowledges my name.
15   He will call upon me, and I will answer him;
I will be with him in trouble,

I will deliver him and honor him.
16   *With long life will I satisfy him*
and show him my salvation."

Climb Every Mountain

*C*hurches, mosques, temples, pews, prayer circles: I've witnessed and experienced firsthand how these traditional sites of worship are powerful places of refuge and peace for so many military moms. For other moms, the natural world serves as an equally potent sanctuary, offering an unrivaled larger-than-yourself perspective check and the opportunity to forget, for a moment, the cares of our mundane world. Look no further than a majestic mountain range or a vast expanse of ocean for a reminder that there exists a force much greater than yourself and that man does not have all the answers to everything. Although I often feel humbled when surrounded by the grandeur, the beauty, and the power of the natural world, I almost always feel a simultaneous sense of union or oneness with it, too. Maybe this is what invites the feeling of peace that hiking in the woods or walking along a deserted beach offers to so many.

Caroline is an Army mom who I met through Brendan's ROTC unit. She and her family have looked to the wilderness for renewal ever since her children were young. "We were never in church on

Sunday. It's not that we didn't have faith. It's just that our spirits yearned to be out of doors. We were so recharged by the ocean and the river and the mountains—the mountains, especially—that our car was always packed and ready to go. And now that my son John is deployed, I just ache to be out under the stars. I can't explain it, but I feel so much better knowing I am sleeping under the same stars that he is. And so we camp out at least once a month, and I know that he and I are connected."

I've heard about that feeling of connection under the stars from more than one mother. My sister Mary is now an Army mom. Not long ago she reminded me about the times when we were little that we couldn't afford to stay in motels because our family was so large. "I didn't know that was the reason we camped, though," she confessed with a laugh. "Dad would say, 'Kids, I wonder what the poor people are doing right now,' and I really thought we camped because we were rich. Actually, camping *made* us rich—in family connection, and stories of triumphs over adversity—remember the time we forgot the tent poles?—and in so many ways.

"Now, when my heart aches from missing my son, I can head to the hills. I can imagine him sitting around a fire like me, waking in a cold night and sleeping under the same stars. It gives me comfort and bridges a generation. I like to think Dad is up there watching over him from afar. 'No finer thing you can ever do, son,' the Colonel would be saying to him, 'than sleep under the stars with your men at your side.'"

Sleeping under the same stars. Apart yet together.

Caroline's and Mary's reflections remind me of a beautiful observation that I've heard attributed to various sources, from Native American prayers to Hindu teachings: *We all walk the same earth, breathe the same air, and are warmed by the same sun.* I think the words are meant to remind us that as human beings we are all connected, no matter how different we may seem. And it's true. We are. But since no military mother needs a reminder of how connected she is to her children—our heartstrings stretch as far across the country and around the globe as we need them to—from now on when I think of Caroline's and Mary's words, I will be reminded of my gratitude for the constants in the physical world—the sun and stars above, the earth underfoot—that also connect me to my children every day and night, no matter where in the world they might be.

If the physical world is a source of joy and strength for you, like it is for so many military moms, I urge you to immerse yourself in nature as regularly as possible. Gina remembers that when her son was in flight school, she felt like she was holding her breath for an entire year. Her son had wanted his wings since he was a little boy, and Gina was a basket case whenever she thought about the high stakes of each flight and each check ride; flight school standards are so stringent that every pilot candidate is only a few mistakes away from failing out at any given moment.

"Finally, my husband said, 'That's it. We're going to hike the Grand Canyon,'" Gina told me. "So we did. No cell phones, no communication, and plenty of physical exertion in a place of breathtaking beauty. I could not believe what a blessed relief it was. I learned that I needed to do that more often—just shut down and get away from everything, preferably in the great outdoors. I can't control anything anyway, and nature helps me to remember that."

Karla, a mom I met on the listserv, lives in Minnesota, where her family has a cabin on a lake that she's been going to since she was child. It's a beautiful spot, secluded and full of wildlife. With deer and loons for company, and fishing and blueberry picking—interrupted by the occasional bear sighting—for entertainment, life at the cabin has its own rhythm, one with no resemblance to the rhythm of her normal suburban life. The lake has always meant peace and renewal to Karla, but when Allie, her daughter, deployed, she found herself not wanting to visit the cabin without her. "My mom talked me into it," Karla told me. "She said 'You need some time to rest. You need to go back to a place that's quiet and beautiful and familiar, and that will remind you of a time when you didn't have such big worries.' She was right, as usual. I missed Allie terribly, but I could unwind."

Nature as a place of connection. Nature as a restorative. Nature as a safe haven where we can disconnect from the news and the worries of our everyday lives. Nature as a sacred spot for worship, and for remembering our place in the universe. If the outdoors has been a source of peace and renewal for you, please make sure you spend time in it regularly.

And if you haven't yet discovered nature as a place of refuge and relief from stress, well, maybe it's time to grab a sleeping bag and a water bottle and climb a mountain. I was given the gift of that opportunity when I was sixteen years old and my father was deployed in Vietnam. Sixteen is a difficult age for many girls, a time of vacillation and self-doubt. Add to the normal angst of that period the responsibility of being second-in-command, with six younger siblings, and the challenge of having your dad away fighting a war that many people hated. Sometimes I just wanted to run away from it all and be a silly teenager.

My mother very wisely decided I needed a change a pace, a change of perspective, and some time away. So she sent me off to attend the Colorado Outward Bound Wilderness Survival School, where for twenty-eight days I hiked, climbed, and rappelled in the West Elk Wilderness Area. This adventure may not sound out-of-the-ordinary today, when so many people are engaged in extreme sports, but back then it was definitely an unusual way for a teenage girl to spend a summer. In fact, it was a challenge just to assemble the gear; I had to buy men's hiking boots because I couldn't find any that were made for women.

In the beginning, hiking up and down the massive mountains was so physically challenging I just stumbled through the days and fell into my sleeping bag at night. But as I got stronger, I began to notice the aspen leaves as they quivered on the trees, turning from green to golden yellow, and the smell of the pines as we gained elevation. I learned to distinguish the calls of different birds and to appreciate the singing of the tree frogs. And when we climbed a knife ridge, even though my heart felt like it was pounding out of my chest with fear, the unlimited views were worth the exertion and the risk. Row after row of peaks marched into the horizon—some jagged and rocky, some glimmering and shimmering and soft with snow. I learned to listen to the silence and hear, and to see what I had not previously seen.

That time scrambling up and down mountains offered me the refuge I needed so desperately. I was away from telephones, newspapers, and television—anything that might remind me of the war—and freed from the burdens of helping my mom on the home front. My nightmares about losing my dad vanished, and I began to feel calmer and happier. Now, even in the loneliest of times, majestic vistas can replenish my spirit, and mountains and pine trees translate into recharging for me. Whenever I find a peak to climb, I head up—even if I have to cover part of the path by car these days.

There is nothing like climbing a mountain—literally rising above it all—to restore and redirect your thoughts, and to give you a new perspective. When you're on the mountainside, at the mercy of the rain and wind and rocks and heat and ice and critters, there is no time for self-doubt or negativity. All you can do is keep moving forward and keep looking up.

Keep looking up. Is there a clearer, truer bit of advice for military moms than this? I'd be hard pressed to find one. Perhaps this is why nature is such a refuge for so many military moms—it forces you to *keep looking up:* to the stars, the sun, the moon. To the leaves rustling in the wind on a wooded path. To the sometimes swift, sometimes lazy movement of clouds in the sky. To the mountaintops. To the heavens.

Nourish Your Soul

You can't stop the clock. That axiom is repeated again and again at the US Naval Academy as plebes embark on Plebe Summer. The words are meant to be encouraging, although they never sounded exactly that way to me. But I get the idea. By the time Jordan started the long hot summer, I knew all too well that the four hours between breakfast and lunch might feel like nothing less than an eternity, but the truth is that time marches on no matter how miserable we are. And since time marches on, it is inevitable that at some point, the misery will end.

The same holds true when we contemplate a deployment or any other fraught time. It seems like the clock *has* stopped. The calendar pages that once flipped with regularity, or even too quickly, now remain stubbornly fixed in place. And it gets harder and harder to hold your breath when those pages just don't move. But the danger of measuring your life in time—Plebe *Summer, four weeks* of training, *nine-month* deployment—is that it can become all too easy to spend your days in a kind of limbo, a purgatory in which real living is suspended.

So what can we military moms do to be sure we are actually living our lives in meaningful ways, and not just going through the motions, watching the minutes tick by?

We have to nourish our souls. What does this mean? It means showing ourselves the same extraordinary kindnesses that we would show to our best friend. It means listening attentively to what our bodies and minds need (and I do mean need, not necessarily want) and generously giving ourselves those things. It means developing an acute awareness of the impact our surroundings and relationships have on our attitudes and outlooks.

Allow me to explain. I've discovered that taking care of myself and my world in an intentional way helps to fill an expanse of time that may, at the outset, seem interminable. One way I do this is to try to make the world a more physically beautiful place. During one of Jordan's deployments, I planted a blue and gold garden in honor of his Naval service. Designing the garden and then creating and maintaining it was incredibly satisfying. Planting and taking care of the flowers were rhythmic acts that I found calming, and every time I looked out the window, the rich colors of the garden gave me pleasure. Best of all, as I tracked the garden's growth and progress, I could track the progress of my son's deployment. The more things grew—even the weeds—the closer he was to coming home.

And then there's knitting, of course, which I swear must be one of the most cathartic activities known to mankind. I love the sensory nature of the act—the soft wool in my hands, the sound of the clicking needles—as well as its practicality—scarves and sweaters to keep my loved ones warm! And of course, there's the great satisfaction of creating things of beauty. An added bonus (not that I need one) is that as with the garden, I can watch a project progress and know that as rows pile on and sleeves emerge and borders take shape, my child is closer and closer to coming home.

I have plenty of creative Sisters right there with me. Some mothers quilt, some mothers paint. Clarissa scrapbooks. Those collections of photos that she's never had time to organize have become her path to communion with her daughter. As she creates page after page of family history, she has the sense of watching a movie of her daughter's life unfolding. "I see her baby face turning to one of resolute determination in the softball field. Some nights I cry, and other nights I laugh. Each page that is completed means we're one step closer to her homecoming. I can't wait to show the book to her."

When our kids are young, many of us mothers are so busy that we don't take time for our creative endeavors. Although she was an accomplished artist, Sandy, a Navy mom, stopped painting years ago when her three toddlers overtook her studio. As her nest emptied and she began to prepare for her son's upcoming deployment, she decided to pull out her paints and brushes again. "I realized it was time for me to get re-engaged with my passion. I remembered what you told me about your knitting, and I decided to immerse myself in something creative to fill the emptiness. I am so thrilled to be painting again! The time just flies when I am at the easel, and I know that this will make all the difference for me when John is away."

My friend Maria realized during her daughter's deployment that in order to nourish her soul, she needed to find a different daily rhythm. A slower, more intentional one. She turned to simple, almost monastic practices, somewhat as if she were living in an abbey or an ashram. For her, the ritual of going through her day on a completely predictable schedule is very comforting; it makes her feel in control when there is so much she cannot control. She says, "It's kind of like the 'pray' part in *Eat, Pray, Love*. I move through the day very purposefully and with order, and do everything in a routine. It is very calming. It keeps me centered while my daughter is in dangerous places and I can't talk to her."

When Maria tells me this, I look at her quizzically, and she laughs. She knows what my look means. For some of us, a simple, predictable schedule is the last thing we want. Instead, we look to fill our days with frenetic activity. We keep busy. We keep moving. Our need for go-go-go soul nourishment manifests in many ways. Some of my friends' ambitious baking projects would put Betty Crocker to shame. Other friends might scrub their tubs spotless and mop their floors to a high sheen, as if they were in the finals for the Cleanest House in the Neighborhood award. For the record, I was out of *that* contest in the preliminaries—a fact I would have felt bad about had it not been for a military mom friend who told me: "I hold myself together by focusing on taking care of people. My family, my community, my church, my military sisters. That means something has to give. So at my house, the dust bunnies have grandchildren and I don't care." I figure that if she doesn't care about dust bunnies and dust bunny descendants, I don't either.

The point is that there is no right way to pace yourself or fill your day. But whether you choose simple, calming rituals or a jam-packed schedule, you must be sure to make *you* a priority. You cannot let your own health and well-being suffer because your children are in challenging or dangerous situations. Me? I know I need to get plenty of rest; exhaustion has a way of making me (and most of us) more volatile and less happy. What about you? Do you also need to get a good night's sleep in order to be most present for your loved ones? Or is it a good long morning run that you can't function without, or a yoga class? Do you need an hour at the end of every day to swing on your back porch and be alone with your thoughts? An extended walk with the dog? A morning meditation? Whatever those things are that help you feel happy and well, *do them.*

How else to nourish your soul? It may help to remind yourself regularly that you belong to an extended community of families who are sharing the same challenges and sacrifices that you are. *You are not alone* in what you are going through. Your Sisters, and the rest of your family, are there for you in whatever way you need them to be, whether it's encouragement, a helping hand, or a shoulder to cry on.

So many moms I know say that actively reminding themselves of all the *good* in the world is a calming, energizing practice. This is especially essential if your child is in a combat zone. It's easy to be sucked under by stories in the news—or stories from your deployed child—of the pain and the brutality that exist in war-ravaged places. But when you are at home and can do nothing about the violence and the ugliness far away, I believe that it's better just to focus on making your own small corner of the universe a better and happier place. I can promise you with complete certainty that your anxiety and anguish will not help your child. Instead, you can choose to be a point of light and to let your light shine on your immediate surroundings. You will be happier, and so will those around you. And maybe, just maybe, if that light shines brightly enough, a small amount of it will radiate out to wherever your loved one is.

To keep that light shining brightly, many moms and families I know accept that it requires a certain degree of protection and shielding from all the bad news, scary images, and alarmist headlines that threaten to overwhelm us every day. Additionally, some parents choose to avoid any potentially upsetting books and movies. Mike, an Explosive Ordnance Device (EOD) dad, recalls watching the Academy Award-winning film *The Hurt Locker*. He realized too late that it was a huge mistake, given that the movie is about an elite squad of soldiers whose job it is to disarm bombs in the heat of battle; the vivid recreation of his son's experience hit way too close to home. "It was very well done," he said, "but I don't know when the nightmares will stop."

Mike is not alone. When my neighbor Jana's Army son was sent to Afghanistan, she thought it would be a good idea to become educated about this "new" war zone. "I started my reading with *The Kite Runner*. Bad choice. I couldn't make it through." She tried other books only to find the same thing; she'd get as far as the first or second chapter, and then she'd stop. The details were just too brutal and upsetting. "I finally decided I didn't need all that information. I just needed to focus on reminding my son that home was still here, and that there were still good people in the world."

I know many military parents who, like Mike and Jana, make it a practice to avoid all contemporary war movies and books. If you find that eliminating anxiety-inducing pop-culture experiences protects you from negative thought patterns, nightmares, and "what-if" mental spirals, then by all means eliminate those experiences. And don't let anyone tell you that you're just pulling the wool over your own eyes or choosing to remain naïve about the world around you—avoiding unnecessary upset is an exercise in taking care of yourself. So go ahead. Protect yourself.

On the other hand, I once asked a friend—one of the strongest women I know, someone I have never seen even *flinch* when the going gets tough—how she maintains her equilibrium, and she replied, "When I feel myself slipping, I get out the Patton movie and I watch him give that speech. It just makes me want to stand at attention and salute." I love the thought of her saluting; the image always makes me want to laugh. But the point is this: that particular war movie inspires her, and she views that climactic speech as her own personal pep talk. She has figured out exactly what she needs in order to restore her inner strength, and she gives it to herself.

*A*nd while we're on the subject of things that restore us versus things that we want to keep at a distance, what about those negative, pessimistic people in our lives? You know who I mean: those energy-vampire friends who leave you feeling depleted and cynical. I've found that one of the most effective ways to nourish my soul during tough times is to steer clear of them and of all toxic relationships. I know that sometimes it's tough to decline that lunch date or not pick up that call, but when you know the interaction will suck your energy and leave you worse for the wear, it's okay. In fact, it's for the best. And don't be shy about talking with friends about what behaviors and actions they are doing right—and wrong. Marine mom Juanita speaks about the time when one of her well-intentioned friends sent her a Facebook message saying *I saw what happened in Afghanistan yesterday. I'm praying for you.* "I had to tell her to stop it because she scared the crap out of me. Exactly what was the specific thing that had happened that made her pray for me? I went crazy searching the internet to try to find out." Sometimes it's better to simply say, "I'm thinking of you."

Now what if—and take a good, honest look at yourself here— *you* are that negative, toxic energy vampire? How do you change your negative mental feedback loop so that you aren't the one that friends and family avoid? If you're truly stuck in a place of anxiety, worry, and negativity, you might consider seeking counseling from a pastor, priest, or therapist. There's nothing wrong with asking for help when you need it. In fact, it's a healthy, mature thing to do, even if it's hard. Even if asking for help is not what you normally do.

In the meantime—and admittedly, it sounds a bit trite, but I truly believe this—it helps to focus on the positive, not the negative. Sarah, the mom of an Air Force pilot, found a beautiful way to do this. After moping around for a while following her son's deployment, she realized that being depressed didn't do him any good, and that in fact, if she was depressed, it would be just one more thing for him to worry about. So she started a joy journal. Every day she looked for one thing that she could find joy in. Some days were harder than others; it takes real discipline to find joy when we don't feel joyous. But Sarah's persistence paid off. "It's surprising how something as little as keeping this journal made such a big difference in my outlook. I had been dreading this time so much, but—and this may sound strange—instead it became a time of inner refreshment."

Wow. I'll have what she's having.

Amy is a Coast Guard mom. When her son was deployed to Afghanistan, she was completely taken aback. She had no idea that the Coast Guard ever went anywhere near Afghanistan, but in these days of joint assignments, the unthinkable happened, and it sent her into a real funk. She cried a lot and became extremely irritable. When she saw that her fear was affecting her younger children, who were becoming anxious and worried themselves, she knew that she needed to get a grip. Amy decided that she and the kids could make her older son's period of deployment into a time of exploration rather than a time of fear. They got a map and learned more about Afghanistan. They prepared Afghan food and read books—non-threatening, non-violent books—about the culture. At Christmas they donated a goat to a village. All of these things made them feel a lot better. "In a funny way, we felt like we were somehow helping him get his job done."

We hold ourselves together by focusing on good things. On doing good things, on seeing good things, on thinking about good things. We try to be a voice of optimism, reminding our children—in chatty e-mails and newsy letters—that positive, happy things are happening here at home. That there are still places on the earth where people are kind, and children are cared for, and democracy works. We do the things that make home a place of respite when our kids finally get back.

I am lucky to have Courtney to remind me, with patient regularity, that 90 percent of the things we worry about never happen, and the other 10 percent—well, we can't control them anyway. When I stay focused on the positive rather than worrying about all the bad things that might happen, stressful times are so much easier to bear.

By practicing visualization, Sheila, the mother of one of my son-in-law's Air Force classmates, focuses on the positive, too. "Every night I visualize my son coming home. I see him landing his airplane at the air base. My family is all there with banners. I'm standing with the camera so I can take photos of my daughter-in-law and grandson as they greet Tim. I see it all so clearly—the balloons, the smiles, the joyous reunion. I hold tight to these thoughts. No matter what, I don't let go."

I don't let go, either. I hold fast to my children's dreams, the ones that surfaced long ago and the ones that they've worked so hard to achieve: the dreams to make a difference in the world, to be a force for good, to serve their country. Whenever I can, I immerse myself in the positive. I look upward and outward rather than inward or down. I look forward rather than backward. I do my best to keep my light shining bright so that they can keep theirs bright, too, as they continue to make the world a better place.

Sandals on the Ground

_F_aith. Nature. Soul nourishment. _Information._

Yes, sometimes there's information that we want to avoid. Some of us prefer to stay far away from those all-too-realistic books and movies that spell out the dangers and hardships of life in a combat zone in harrowing detail. And some of us have learned that the news we get on radio, television, or from newspapers is not always our friend, especially when reports are inaccurate and we later discover we've been terrified for hours or days for no good reason.

But sometimes information is a godsend.

A major challenge for military moms is the great _mystery_ of our child's deployment and military life. What do they do, exactly, during deployment? Are they in constant danger? How much do they worry about the danger? What do they fear? What are they thinking about? Do they have friends? Do they miss us? What do they eat? Do they like the packages I send? Do they meet locals?

All of the unknowns—so, so many unknowns—can rattle around in our brains and drive us crazy. The last thing we want to do is bombard our children with incessant questions, but sometimes we need information—any information, even just a nugget—to keep us from jumping to the wrong conclusions and assuming the worst.

Through a series of circumstances I couldn't have possibly predicted just a year earlier, in the summer of 2010 I found myself moving to Kabul for ten months to teach in the only coed school in Afghanistan. To others it may have appeared like a totally off-the-wall decision, but in fact, it didn't seem that way to me at all. Courtney's job had him based in Kabul, and I was becoming increasingly lonely in my oh-so-quiet house. I also realized that I wanted to be serving a larger purpose, like my kids were. If I could have some sort of positive influence on the children of Afghanistan, who in turn might have some sort of positive influence on their fellow Afghans in the future—well, then, perhaps my time in Kabul would be worth it. And maybe, just maybe, I could glean some useful information about deployment in that war-torn country. So I was on a reconnaissance mission of sorts.

I took away from my experiences in Afghanistan lessons that were both practical and eye-opening about what life is like for many of our deployed troops. As they say, knowledge is power, and the knowledge I gained while on the ground has been an incredible power in holding me together in the years since. I hope, dear Sister, that my sandals-on-the-ground experience will answer a few of your questions about deployment, and help to hold you together, too.

It was on a blazing hot day in July of 2010 that I found myself headed toward Kabul at twenty-nine thousand feet. As the pilot's wife, I had been upgraded to first class for my flight from Dubai, and

I was treated to a level of respect unparalleled by that on any flight I'd ever taken before. The fact that I was going to live and teach in Kabul was astonishing to the Afghan crew, who just couldn't comprehend why an affluent (in their eyes) Westerner whose country was not ravaged by war—a pilot's wife, no less—would make such a choice. They plied me with tea, cakes, and anything I wanted. But I was mostly oblivious to the crew's kind offers, and to the other passengers in first class—the Afghan businessmen seated nearby in their shiny suits and pointy-toed leather shoes, and the contractors whose cargo pants and utility vests, worn no matter what the occasion, announced their profession.

My face was pressed against the window of the B-767 as I contemplated the changing terrain and my changing future. Below, the deep-blue waters of the Straits of Hormuz, which separates the Arabian Peninsula from Iran, were receding as we entered Iranian air space. Forty-five minutes later we crossed into Afghanistan. From the air, the southwestern part of that vast country resembles the endlessly arid landscape of Arizona and New Mexico. We flew over Kandahar and continued north, where the terrain rapidly became more rugged, and in the mountain ranges below it became hard to discern any signs of life beyond the occasional walled compound. As we approached Kabul, strategically situated in a valley surrounded by a ring of mountains and, at six thousand feet, one of the highest capital cities in the world, I could see the majestic Hindu Kush rising to the north, their snowy peaks glistening in the sun. We began our descent, and Courtney steered us through a notch between two mountains as if he were casually threading a needle.

I cleared immigration and security alone—Courtney, as the pilot, took a different route—and the stares directed at me were so intense that I almost felt assaulted. I tried to avert my eyes as much as possible, and kept adjusting and readjusting my headscarf. Maybe I had left some small bit of flesh unacceptably exposed? But no, I was a woman who was apparently traveling alone, a blonde no less (in Kabul, it's acceptable—strangely—to show your bangs), and that was reason enough for the staring. As I navigated the lines and people pushed against me and men tried to grab my luggage to shake me down for tips, my anxiety skyrocketed. Thank God the unflappable Courtney was waiting for me on the other side of customs. An hour later we arrived at the school in western Kabul where I was to be living and teaching. When I logged on to the Internet later that day, I noticed that Brendan, my Army son, had the ultimate Facebook status of the day: *Four military kids all in the USA. Mom and Dad in Afghanistan. Just a normal American family.*

Courtney stayed with me for two days at the school, which with its walls, gates, and security guards, felt like a prison of sorts to me, and then it was time for him to get back to work. I seriously considered climbing into the taxi alongside him. *Why in the world did I trade the comfort and familiarity of home for life in this war-ravaged city?* I moaned to myself, as I had been doing pretty much ever since I'd landed. But no one in my family had ever quit anything, so I couldn't start now.

And so began my ten-month reconnaissance mission in Afghanistan.

Beyond my desire to spend time with Courtney, acquire some intel, and do some good in the world, why in the world *had* I left my comfortable life in Ohio? The answers to that question go all the way back to September 11, 2001. One of the seemingly infinite ripple effects of the devastation wrought on that day was that the airline industry in the United States suffered wide-scale losses. When US Airways, Courtney's employer for twenty-eight years, declared bankrupcy, it liquidated all of its pilots' pensions. Our retirement savings—and those of approximately six thousand other pilots—vanished as we all became uninsured creditors.

And there was another issue looming over us, too. Courtney would be required by United States law to retire as an airline pilot in 2007. At the time, I was working for the county on child and family issues, and there was no way that my salary was going to support us in our golden years now that our savings had disappeared. So Courtney began looking for international flying jobs. Later, Congress would raise the mandatory retirement age of all US pilots to sixty-five, but Courtney had already moved on.

In November of 2008 he received a call to interview for a job in Afghanistan as a B-737 pilot. Two weeks later, after a short phone interview, he found himself in London flying the simulator. Soon he called home with the news: he had gotten the job, which, it turns out, was more than just a flying job. He was one of ten pilots from the West hired to reinvent the Afghan airline Safi Airways. With so many contractors and embassy officials traveling to Kabul, there was a tremendous need for a quality passenger airline, and Safi needed a complete overhaul to meet that need. The challenge was enormous, which is probably why the opportunity appealed to my adventurous husband. Courtney flew straight to Dubai from London to participate in the rebuilding of the airline from the ground up.

I worried about him constantly. Geographically, Kabul is a dangerous airport to fly into and out of, and learning that Courtney was using his Vietnam War experience as a C-130 pilot to teach his fellow pilots rocket-avoidance procedures did not add to my happiness. Beyond that, the house was far too silent. After years of praying for an occasional moment of peace and quiet, my life was now too full of it.

Six months later, at Katrina's graduation from the Naval Academy—a giddily happy occasion with Courtney home and all of the siblings together—my better half regaled us with story after story about the great people of Afghanistan and their warm hospitality. Sitting at a happily raucous celebratory dinner with my family one night, I had a revelation: I should visit my husband in Kabul to see his situation for myself, and maybe then I'd stop worrying so much. When I mentioned this idea out loud, my kids were not surprised. After all, this was the mom who had hiked forty miles on the Appalachian Trail to celebrate her fortieth birthday, and who had run (okay, shuffled) the Marine Corps Marathon twice.

So I headed to Afghanistan in June of 2009 to get a sense of Courtney's new life, hoping that the experience would help to calm my fears. At the time, I had no idea that I would end up moving there, and that this was actually the start of a prolonged information-gathering mission. But in fact, the brief trip was my first step toward having sandals on the ground.

After my visit, I returned to Ohio to prepare for another year of school. By now I was teaching high school science in my local school district with the ultimate goal of pursuing a doctorate in education focusing on school and community partnerships. I liked my work as a teacher, but as the summer progressed into fall and I missed my husband and children and nephew more and more, I realized that teaching wasn't going to be enough for me at this juncture of my life. At least, teaching in *Ohio* wasn't going to be enough for me. Perhaps there was another place I could make more of a difference, a place where I could see Courtney and continue to learn about a country that some of my children might be deploying to before long? Well, yes, as it happened, I could think of just such a place. And so I started looking for a teaching job in Kabul.

Six months after arriving at my decision to move, Courtney and I pulled through the heavily guarded gates to my new home, an English-speaking school for Afghan children and the children of NGO and aid workers. I was situated in a spacious house with six other women, most of whom were no older than my kids, and given the first floor bedroom so that Courtney could stay with me when his flying schedule allowed. In fact, that rarely happened. We were only eight miles apart, but security concerns, street-clogging traffic, and Courtney's frequent travel would make it impossible to get together with any regularity, although we had no way of knowing that at the time.

Within the compound I could move about freely, but that was not the case beyond those walls and guarded gates. None of the live-in staff or teachers could ever go anywhere unaccompanied, nor could we drive. Even when we were permitted to leave the grounds—if there had been an "incident" in the city, we were confined to the compound—we were very limited as to where we could go. And of course we always had to wear our *chadars*, or headscarves. "Chadar up!" we used to say to each other, thrilled to be getting a change of pace, whenever we prepared to leave school grounds.

Within the first few days after Courtney's departure, I was assaulted by bedbugs (one eye so swollen that I couldn't open it) and Kabul stomach (with vendors using open sewer water to rinse off road dust, illness was inevitable no matter how much we cleaned our food). And as I adjusted to life in a city in a war zone, I began to learn some valuable military mom lessons.

LESSON #1
YOU DON'T HAVE TO WORRY ALL THE TIME.

Things are often not as bad as you fear. One day shortly after I arrived, a tribal uprising in the streets directly outside of the school had me sheltering in place in my classroom. I called Courtney in Dubai, sobbing, and naturally he was alarmed. I told him I'd call back as soon as we'd gotten the all clear, and then sat weeping with a coworker for the next hour, wondering, for the umpteenth time, why I had ever decided to come to Kabul. When I finally went to a neighboring room to seek new word on our status, I saw teachers walking freely around the courtyard. My coworker and I had misinterpreted our directions; we had been meant to remain on school grounds, not huddled in our classroom. In my relief, I forgot to call Courtney back, and I had turned off my phone.

Several hours later, I realized that I hadn't checked back in with him and I called with profuse apologies. In the years that have followed, my children have deployed over and over again. During the early deployments, if the slightest *breeze*—not to mention news report or ambiguous e-mail—suggested that one of them might be in danger, I would hold my breath, wring my hands, and allow my mind to indulge in worst-case-scenario thinking. With each passing hour, minute, second that I didn't hear from them, I slipped further down the rabbit hole of negative what-ifs. But eventually, I trained myself to remember that afternoon in Kabul, when I had been frightened for an hour and then was fine. Courtney, far from the action, had worried for three or four times as long.

Try to limit your worry.

LESSON #2
DEPLOYMENT IS BORING AND LONELY.

The military personnel I came to know at Camp Eggers, the base in Kabul, had Friday mornings off. Every other day, almost without exception, they worked twelve to fourteen hours. When they did have time off, there was no place to go, so they tended to keep working. The same was true for us at the school, although to a lesser extent, where the days blended into each other in a haze of work and missing home, family, and the freedom to move around without restriction. After a while, this routine inevitably became excruciatingly boring.

Then the boredom would vanish when rocket attacks, suicide bombers, and shooting in the streets threatened our safety and forced us to shelter in place. There's an old aviation saying, modified slightly here, which I now fully understand: *Deployment can be hours of boredom interrupted by moments of sheer terror.* Which means that yes, after the sheer terror, the boredom returns.

Those who are boots on the ground, going house to house and interacting with the local population, experience much less boredom. But they certainly share the second aspect of all deployments: loneliness. You may bond with your battle buddies in profound and lasting ways, but nothing replaces the love of the family and friends who have shared your history and your life.

I handled my boredom and loneliness by staying in motion, which just happens to be one of the ways I handle my children's deployments when I'm at home, too. I kept busy with classwork and I knit, knit, knitted. I took the ballet and tap classes that the principal's wife was offering and helped with costumes for the yearly ballet recital given by Afghanistan's sole dance academy. (The challenges of designing and producing two hundred culturally appropriate ballet costumes—ballet without tights and tutus?—cannot be overstated.)

A lot of military personnel handle their time deployed by staying in motion, too. Gyms and workout centers on base are frequently packed at all times of the day and night. All this working out is not the narcissistic, self-centered occupation it may seem like to some. When your physical world has pretty much shrunk to the size of your base, to move is to keep your mind occupied, away from the thoughts that might overwhelm you with longing for home. On top of that, exercise releases all sorts of feel-good endorphins that zing around your mind and body, inevitably lifting your spirits. Even I acquired the workout habit, joining some of the younger school staff in a rigorous physical fitness program. And I assure you that if I, a person who *hates* working out, was spending an hour and a half five times a week sweating through the P-90X routine in order to keep the loneliness and boredom at bay, the loneliness and boredom of my "deployment" were extreme. (Full disclosure: by the end of my time in Kabul I still couldn't do half of the moves, but I kept attempting them anyway just to be part of the group.)

As tough as the loneliness and the boredom were at the time, though, from the current perspective of a mom who can't help but worry about her kids, I'm glad to know that these challenges, rather than other more dangerous ones, are two of the biggest and most common trials faced by many of our deployed young men and women.

LESSON #3
WHILE YOU ARE WORRYING ABOUT THEM,
THEY ARE WORRYING ABOUT YOU.

*E*arly on, I realized that I'd need a lot more than teaching, dance classes, and costume creation to get me through my time in Kabul. Fortunately, I knew just where to go to get what I needed: Camp Eggers in general, and the chapel there in particular. Being surrounded by young men and women from all branches of the service—just like my own children!—nourished my mother's heart. Naturally, I adopted anyone I could, hugging the young people around me and trying to dispense as much mom energy as I could. I listened to their concerns, cried over their losses with them, and celebrated with people as they prepared to ship home. The time I spent on base was a privilege I wouldn't trade for anything.

And as if all that weren't enough, there were also the chapel services, which never failed to renew me. Picture a large olive-drab tent with rows of folding chairs filled with men and women from every service branch. With so many guardsmen and reservists deploying, a surprising number of those in uniform were older than you might expect. As the military chaplains—"Chaps"—greeted everyone, you could almost see people's cares falling away. But it was during prayer request time that I was always moved so deeply. Men and women would share their concerns, and they were always about home. "My boy blew out his knee playing football and he's having surgery and I can't be there," one might say. Or "My husband is really struggling with the kids," or "My mom is sick," or "The new baby's not sleeping and my wife is exhausted." The stresses of their jobs certainly weighed on people, but worrying about loved ones at home seemed to me to be the bigger challenge for most people, and the faces of even the most hardened warriors would soften as they told me about their families. They would pull out stacks of pictures and show me their wives and kids, their moms and dads.

"Ma'am, I can't wait to tell my mom (or my wife or my girlfriend) that you are here! It will make her feel so much better knowing a grandma is here with us!" they'd tell me.

"Oh, you have no idea how good it makes me feel to be here with you," I'd respond with a huge smile. There is nothing like people who *feel* like family, or remind you of family, or who miss their families just like you're missing yours, to bring you comfort when you're far from home.

You are always on your loved ones' minds.

LESSON #4

THERE IS NO SUCH THING AS TOO MUCH MAIL.

Mail makes a difference. This is something I've been told, something that I've seen, and now that I, too, have felt such happiness and gratitude upon receiving a little piece of home while living in a war zone, something that I've experienced firsthand. Mail is love, and there is no such thing as too much love.

The mail service was close to nonexistent while I was living in Kabul, and I missed those daily deliveries far more than I ever could have imagined. I even missed the bills and the junk mail. I missed anything that disrupted the monotony of our daily routine and relieved the loneliness of being away from all that was familiar. I missed the smells and feel of home, the tastes, and most importantly, the connections. I missed being around people who knew me beyond the context of my job. Mail was the path to all of that. No mail equals no connection.

Occasionally a surprise letter wound its way from the United States to Kabul via who knows what route. I was overjoyed to have it, and the fact that it took three months to reach me was unimportant. The school's Internet connection was also inconsistent, and on some days everyone's e-mail inbox was empty. A long chatty e-mail, when it did eventually arrive, filled with lots of news about dogs and cats and gossip from home and peonies and raspberry yields—well, that erased the gray skies and the concertina wire and gave me moments of almost giddy happiness. And when the bandwidths inexplicably opened and I was, through the miracle of Skype, able to see my grandbaby's face and hear her cry, I felt nothing less than sheer joy.

On the days when security levels were green and my fellow teachers and I were allowed to make the four-mile trek to Camp Eggers with our Afghan driver, we would hop in the car and head straight there. After navigating the streets of downtown Kabul in our battered vehicle (battered so that it would blend in with all the others), headscarves in place, we would be deposited at the first checkpoint. There we would stand waiting to be cleared while Afghan children tried to sell us scarves or bracelets or gum. Finally we would make it past the first point and on to the next, and then to the next. There was always a period of tension once we arrived at the gates of the base, where we would emerge from the car in order to clear security. Because many attacks happen at the entrances of military facilities, they are dangerous places to be. Once we were identified as Americans, we were allowed to proceed through sandbagged walls to an interior space. There we were approved to move onto the base, where the chaplain would finally meet us. The whole process was anxiety provoking, but I was grateful for the tight security. It meant that my children were protected by stringent safety protocols, too.

First we would go to the Green Beans Café. There we drank American coffee, soaked in the heady aromas of home, and listened to the music—yes, music!—of American soldiers talking. Then the chaplain would take us to his office, and there might be a few care package boxes that had broken open, boxes that had arrived without a specifically named recipient. And he would say, "I thought you might like these." And in one broken-down box there would be some Tootsie Rolls and Snickers bars, a five-pound bag of flour, and some hot chocolate mix; in another there might be some crushed boxes of Pop-Tarts, some chewing gum, and some powdered lemonade. Those boxes meant the comfort of familiar tastes and smells from home. They meant love from home. It didn't matter whether the items were meant for me or not. What the boxes meant was that someone at home cared about others far, far away. And on some cold and dreary days, that caring from home made all the difference.

LESSON #5

IT IS WORTH IT.

As the year progressed, my students did well, and I was enormously gratified to see their advances. But I was worried for them, too. Suicide bombings were a continuing part of our reality. During the ten months that I taught at the school, there were a number of them within the city—one involving a bus carrying Afghan intelligence forces, one in the nearby grocery store that we frequented, and others scattered throughout different neighborhoods.

In February, the beautiful Safi Landmark Hotel suffered its second attack since I had stayed there eighteen months earlier on my first trip to the country. My junior high girls and I heard the bus bomb from our classroom and raced to the window, where we gaped at the rising smoke. Most of the students were sobbing as they pulled out their phones and desperately called home to make sure all family members were safe. *How in the world*, I wondered, *will growing up in a war zone affect these children?*

I am frequently asked, especially by military mothers, what it was like to live in Kabul during such violent and uncertain times. Try as I might to find one, there is no simple answer to that question. It's hard to describe what it's like to sit at a parent–teacher conference and have one of the first women elected to the Afghan Parliament thank you for coming to her country to teach her daughter and her daughter's classmates; it's hard for me to fathom that this woman risked her life for the sake of educating young girls in her country, running a hidden school during the reign of the Taliban, an action that in all likelihood would have led to her execution had it been discovered. And yet here she was, thanking me and all of the other teachers who came to offer their services at her daughter's perfectly legal school.

It's hard to describe what it feels like to have fathers weep, *weep*, in gratitude because you have given their children the gift of education—the gift of hope for the future. Or what it feels like to hear a classroom full of Afghan teenagers recite Teddy Roosevelt's 1910 "Man in the Arena" speech in its entirety, with feeling, and talk about what it means to have the courage to be true to their convictions and to dare to be brave in the face of discouragement. It's hard to describe these people, and these moments, but they made a lasting impression on my heart.

Many of my students still stay in touch with me today. Even in the darkest of times, they remind me of the ways in which their country is fighting to move past tribal differences and work toward a better understanding of what freedom and democracy mean. I know those students, and their families, value the sacrifices of the American sons and daughters who served in Afghanistan in order to bring stability and freedom to their nation, and I know that they will continue to work toward these ends themselves.

I have always been proud to be a military mother, but there are few times in my life when I have been more proud to be so than when I was in Afghanistan. We will never know how many lives have been and will be positively affected by the sacrifices of our nation's best and brightest, but I believe the number is far greater than we imagine, because I believe in the ripple effect. As our children continue to man their stations all over the world, we can never underestimate the power of the beacon of freedom that they represent. In times of trouble, our children are the hope of the world.

For the most part, my days in Kabul now blend together in a surreal haze until I am jolted by a headline or a call from a worried mom. The headlines are almost always upsetting, but the phone calls are often a pleasure.

"My daughter is deploying in a week to Helmand. What can you tell me?" the mom might ask.

And I begin to talk to her about all the wonderful people I met, and I assure her that there will be many people who are grateful that her daughter is there. And we discuss the must-haves in the care packages—baby wipes to fight the dust that permeates everything, and ChapStick, and good-smelling anything. I tell her to write long, newsy letters and e-mails about how the dog is doing and what's happening in town, and to be sure to include all the gossip from church, even though we should never gossip and certainly not about our friends from church!

As I share these bits and pieces of information, I can feel my fellow member of the Sisterhood start to relax a little. Because for mothers, knowledge is power. Knowing just a little bit of what our children will be facing and what we can do to make their lives easier helps to hold us together. And when we can see our children serving not just as warriors but as humanitarians—well, that binds all of us together as people.

The Calling

The world sees a square-jawed, steely-eyed soldier; I see a little boy cuddling kittens under the big oak tree. The world sees an officer with a pistol on her thigh; I see a little girl in pigtails on the swing set. Behind every warrior is a family that loves him or her, and very often a mom who wonders "How did this happen? It seems like yesterday that my little one was in my arms. Now that little one carries arms of his or her own." And when our kids are deployed and we are doing everything we can to hold ourselves together, those images of little boy dimples and little girl grins can sometimes bring us down and cause us to despair. The sweetness and the sense of wonder that shone from their young souls seem like such distant memories.

But if we look deeper and we are true to our memories, and ourselves, we have to acknowledge the passionate, dare-to-be-different kind of kids our youngsters were. The "I'm going to climb the highest tree because I can" kind of kid. The "I'm not afraid of nothin'" kind of kid. The "I'm going to do this even though none of my friends are doing it because it's the right thing to do" kind of kid. The qualities that we have seen all along in our children defined the dreams that have become their destinies. For some, the dream was to soar above the clouds. For others, it was to walk with honor and integrity. Others were drawn to fight for right. They have had to work hard to achieve those dreams, and we have had to work just as hard to let go.

When our children say "I want to go, I *need* to go," we do what we have always done. We help them follow their passions. We support their dreams. We let them fly, even if it means letting them fly into harm's way. And what holds us together—in addition to tremendous pride in our children's choice to serve and joy in seeing our kids develop their talents so fully—is the knowledge that *our children are doing exactly what they were born to do.* It's hard to argue with destiny.

When Sandy's oldest son Eric announced that he was pursuing an appointment to the US Naval Academy, she was not surprised, although other family members were. This was the child who, as a preschooler, could approach a group of boys he'd never met on a city playground, persuade one of them to give him his toy gun, and be brought fully into the day's game within minutes. This was the child who had a passionate interest in twentieth-century military history and preferred watching episodes from the Time Life History Series over almost any other television show. The boy who insisted on heading to the barbershop as soon as summer break began so that he could get his Chesty Puller haircut—and who then had to educate his parents about that most-decorated Marine. The boy who sheepishly admitted to sleeping on his bed slats, without a mattress, because he had been reading about POWs and wanted to experience their harsh sleeping conditions.

Sandy's father and father-in-law had served in the military, as many in their generation had, but neither Sandy nor her husband considered their family to be a military one. Her husband was somewhat alarmed by Eric's decision to pursue a military career, and when Eric received his appointment, his two younger siblings asked Sandy, horrified, if she was actually going to "let" him go to Annapolis.

"My answer to them today is the same as it was then: 'It's not my choice, it's his. I will not clip his wings and I won't ever discourage you from following your dreams, either.'"

That didn't stop her from studying Eric intently; on every visit she was able to make to the Yard that first year, she searched for cracks in his armor, fearing that he was secretly miserable. "But he never let me see him sweat, and refused to allow me to wallow in any Navy Mom fretting. 'It's just like any other college, Mom,' he would say, brushing off anything that sounded even faintly like concern or praise."

Sure, she'd think, *it's just like any other college where uniforms are mandatory, leave is limited, and communication is scarce.* But as she has watched his natural leadership abilities develop, she has become more and more certain in the rightness of this path for him.

When Sandy's son started considering different career options within the military, including Special Forces and other high-risk directions, she realized that there was never going to be a "safe" or "safer" option of duty for her son, and she realized that she had to let him go at a much deeper lever than she already had.

"My son's calling has required a deeper commitment to my own vocation of mothering," she said, talking about the necessity of summoning her profound love for him, again and again, in order to come to peace with the risk-filled path he is following. I see this as another lens on "when they serve, we serve." And we serve on deep, deep levels.

So how does Sandy hold it together through her service? "My first-born always left a large wake behind him, and I have ridden the swells and chops, suspended between his endeavors and my other children's lives, trying to smooth the way enough to keep all of them connected, and keep myself sane. I know that I'm in good company as I find myself riding aft, with so many wise and humble Navy moms. And I know, beyond all doubt, that my son is following his calling. And in that I am blessed."

How, when he announces his intention to pursue a career in the military, do you argue with a young man like Eric whose direction has seemed clear so early in life? And how do you argue with a girl who states her service intentions as a middle schooler, and then demonstrates to everyone around her that she has what it takes to succeed?

"Over and over after she announced her decision to serve her country," Dana told me. "God brought people across her path and mine who would tell me in almost identical words that my child was destined for great things in the military. That she had the ability, the drive, the skills, the intelligence, and the heart to be a Marine Officer. Crusty retired sergeants, current Academy midshipmen, high school fitness coaches, and local active-duty officers from all branches of the military. Again and again they would repeat this to me."

Vickie's years at the Naval Academy prepared her for the rigors of military life, the Marine Basic School fine-tuned her skills, and then everyone's predictions about Vickie came true. She was chosen to be part of an elite band of women working quietly to advance the mission of the Corps in their overseas duties. She was handpicked for this job, plucked out of her original assignment. She hadn't even known that the squad existed; if she had, Vickie said, she would have begged to be part of it. But she didn't have to beg. The job came to her.

And when all of the preparation for this assignment was complete, Dana found herself saying goodbye to her daughter on a tarmac in the middle of the night surrounded by other families bidding farewell to their loved ones, too. "I wanted to take photos but was told this was not allowed. There were the Marines with all their gear. And mommies opening strollers, and toddlers in pajamas thrilled to be up in the middle of the night. Pregnant bellies. Newborn babies being delicately and oh-so-dearly held by the uniformed family member, who was trying to drink in every smell, every single second of that experience, knowing that it would have to be held in memory for the months and months ahead."

Dana was not crying, although she had thought she would be. And she was not sad, although she had thought she would be. And to her great amazement, she was not frightened, either. As she looked into her daughter's face when they said their goodbyes, she saw the focus, determination, and grit that had seemed to be present in her daughter since birth—and yet those qualities had been enhanced somehow, solidified and polished. It was the first time Dana had seen that particular look on Vickie's face, and she knew she would savor it the entire time her daughter was gone.

How was Dana feeling at that moment of goodbye? "If I ever had any doubt that this was indeed part of God's plan for my girl, there was none now. She not only met every training challenge along the way, she went beyond what she needed to do. This feels so right. I am at peace," Dana wrote in her journal at the time. "And I rest in the calm of *yes*."

Of course, it's hard to hold onto those moments of total peace indefinitely. What holds Dana together through the months of deployment and the months of reintegration are the memories of that peacefulness, and the faith that her girl is doing exactly what she is supposed to be doing. For all of the worries and all of the fears, deep down she rests in that calm of *yes*.

Sometimes our kids possess all of the qualities that make them such excellent candidates for the military, and then they have an experience that seals the deal, if only in parental retrospect. As I've already shared, our family has always loved the great outdoors, and the kids hiked up mountains with Courtney starting at a very young age. When she was fourteen, Katrina decided she wanted to climb to the base camp of Mount Everest—and so she did, with Courtney, when she was sixteen. By the end of the expedition—which, to this mother's chagrin, included an ascent of the treacherous Khumbu Icefall—the Sherpas had taken to fondly calling her *Sherpina* rather than Katrina. Her experiences in Nepal changed the way she looked at the world. Later, as part of a longer essay, she wrote the following:

The sacrifices of past Americans are what have made the United States the greatest country on earth. As a child I did not really understand what that meant. It took a trip outside my comfort zone to discover what freedom and "the greatest country" really mean. In high school, I went on a month-long expedition to the Base Camp of Everest, with a crew that was committed to building a school for the Nepalese Sherpa children. In the streets of Katmandu, and in the mountains surrounding Everest, I got my first taste of a third world country, and what poverty and civil unrest really feel and look like. I started the trip as a typical 16-year-old, and returned grateful I wasn't living under a tarp or begging in the street. I didn't know why I was so blessed to have been born an American, but I did know that I wasn't going to take it for granted. I needed to give back to the country that had given so much to me.

As a parent, how do you argue with gratitude and a commitment to giving back?

*M*elissa's son knew he wanted to be a SEAL by the middle of his teenage years. He attended the Naval Academy, and during his four years there his parents had the opportunity to become more and more accustomed to the idea that he was headed in this demanding and dangerous direction. Then he was accepted into the SEAL program and they had two additional years, the length of the SEAL training, to accept and come to peace with it.

By the time their son graduated from SEAL school, both of his parents fully understood that Sven was doing what he was called to do in this lifetime. The graduation itself was a time of pride and celebration for them as they honored their son's tremendous accomplishment; on average, only 20 percent of those who start it complete the rigorous two-year program. Their happiness for their son was tempered by the knowledge that he would now be leaving safe harbor and heading into perilous waters, but they'd had long enough to accept the rightness of his choice that their fears and concerns did not overpower their pride and their joy.

Not all parents were so lucky. "I met two sets of parents at graduation," Melissa told me, "one set from Kansas and another from Nebraska. Their sons had enlisted and been accepted for SEAL training at the end of their twelve-week basic training. Those parents were almost in shock," she said. "I'd had six years to get used to the idea that this was my son's calling, but they were still coming to terms with it. I tried to help them understand that I couldn't imagine my son being happy doing anything else, as scary as that might sound. And I'm sure the same is true of their sons, too. You don't make it through Special Forces training unless it's where you're supposed to be.

"I *know* Sven is where he is supposed to be. And that knowledge gives me peace of mind even when I don't hear from him, and even when I know he is in harm's way."

Knowing that our children are following their destinies makes it so much easier to accept the difficult things that they do. I am proud that my children have felt the calling to serve. I am in awe of their willingness to step forward. We never want our loved ones in the line of fire, but we *do* want them to be all that they can be. It's a tough place for a mother's heart. And even though there are times I want to wrap my arms around my kids' legs and drag them back into the house, I hold myself back. I love my children too much to interfere with their destinies.

As I think about the many, many things that sustain and restore our spirits, I am grateful all over again for the blessings of this life. What holds us together? Faith. Pride. Knitting needles. Mountains. Stars. Scrapbooks. Information. To Do lists. Deep breathing.

Community. Forgiveness. Optimism. Knowing that our children are following their destinies. *Love.*

These are the things that sustain us. These are what hold us together.

Then I heard the voice of the Lord saying,
"Whom shall I send? And who will go for us?"
And I said, "Here am I. Send me!"
Isaiah 6:8

Sacrifice

Saying Goodbye
Again and Again

$\mathcal{I}$ wish the scene were as tidy and sweet as one from an old war movie. In fact, in my mind's eye, I can see it playing out in gauzy Technicolor. There I am, standing on the train platform with a lace handkerchief in my hand, waving daintily as my son sticks his head out of the train window and says with a grin, "I love you, Mom. You and dad take care of yourselves, and I'll be home before you know it!" And then the train chugs a little faster, picking up speed until it disappears into the distance, and my husband and I hold hands as we leave the station platform. A lone tear makes its way down my cheek, but my smile is steady and brave.

No, it doesn't look like that at all; the scene when my son or daughter departs for a deployment is anything but sweet and tidy. Courtney and I go to visit our son or daughter a couple of weeks before he or she leaves. We never wait until the last minute because whoever is being deployed needs to spend that time alone with his or her spouse and children. We usually have a good visit and I keep up the facade that all is normal until we get to the airport for our flight home, and then I go into the bathroom and cry so hard I might throw up. I reemerge and my husband repeats his useless pep talk for the umpteenth time. "Don't worry. He (or she) will be fine." It almost always makes me mad.

"How do you know that?" I snarl. After thirty-five years of marriage, Courtney knows to back away and look for coffee and maybe some chocolate to soothe the savage beast now glowering, or maybe actually growling, at him. We have done this so often that we know our parts in this drama. I act brave. We leave. I fall apart. I take my fear out on my husband. He tries to calm me and cannot. He retreats and returns bearing gifts. And slowly I settle into my deployment mode.

A milder version of this routine actually started long before any of my kids ever deployed. It began when they left for their initial trainings and continued every time they said goodbye after a visit. Even though they weren't yet heading for the front lines of battle, I went through the same roller coaster of emotions, wandering the house feeling forlorn and crying over a stray sock left behind. As each child's training progressed, the risks he or she faced were higher. The roller coaster got steeper and the goodbyes got harder. And then we arrived at the moment when, one by one, they were operationally ready for their first deployment. Each, on the eve of his or her departure, was excited. I was not.

I am not proud of the snarling, glaring, and snapping I do as I adjust to my multiple children's multiple deployments, but I accept that I am off-balance at these moments, and so I cut myself some slack. Plus, misery loves company, and I know I am not the only military mom out there who handles these trying times with less than complete grace. I'd be lying if I said this didn't make me feel at least a *teeny* bit better.

I also know that no matter how calm and unflappable the mother of a deployed child may appear on the outside, her mind is always focused on that part of the world where her child finds him or herself, whether on the ground, in the air, or on or under the high seas.

We all have our habits and rituals, the things we do to help us cope with the anxieties of goodbyes and deployments. One Marine mom I know, Nancy, has a son who has deployed multiple times, often to hot spots. I asked her how she handles his absences.

"I know it sounds superstitious, but I feel like all of my energy goes into keeping Jeff safe. I don't have time for drama, and I can't handle chitter chatter because my mind is on my child. The time he was in Iraq, he was without water, lights, and Christmas gifts. And there's no reason to think that future deployments won't be full of hardship, too. My daughter-in-law usually stays off Facebook while he's gone. It's weird what we do to try to keep our loved ones safe."

I could totally identify with her daughter-in-law deciding to go without Facebook. Most people I know make deals with God when their kids are deployed, or deals with the universe at large, something along the lines of: "If I do this (or don't do that) you'll keep him safe, God, right?" Personally, I've been known to walk three miles every day a child was deployed, no matter how crummy the weather, in one of those "If I do this, maybe you'll do that" deals.

"Last week I was invited to lunch," Nancy continued. "As my friends chatted, all I could think about was the fact that my son was probably heading to another combat zone, and soon. And that it looked like he'd be gone for nine months. I started to cry, and the table became quiet. 'I'm so sorry for you,' they all said. 'I know it must be hard.' And they meant it. But they couldn't really understand.

"I walk around the mall and I know there are others who are feeling the same fear, loneliness, and isolation that I am. I wish I knew who they were so I could give them all a hug. Sometimes you just need someone to put their arms around you and tell you it will be okay. It may never be okay, but. . . ." Her voice trails off.

Another friend told me, "I go into silent mode. No news, no television, no Internet except e-mails." This is from someone who is a CNN junkie. "My son's been on four deployments, and by now I know that if I watch the news and hear the word *Afghanistan* or *casualties*, my heart starts palpitating like crazy. It's like that old saying: No news is good news. If I don't hear it or read about it, surely he must be alright."

You would think by now we would be used to saying goodbye. It's been more than a decade since we started sending our children, born in a time of peace, into combat, and I've had to watch mine deploy time and time again. In truth, my goodbyes started way back when I was a little girl hugging her father as he headed off for yet another assignment, and so the reality of the situation is that I've had more than fifty years of practice. In this case, practice clearly does not make perfect, and even if it did, I'd opt for imperfection, thank you very much.

So let me ask you: How do *you* say goodbye? Have you discovered a way to make it any easier on yourself? Any easier on your kids, or on your partner or spouse, if you have one? I'm asking because I've come to believe that the only way we can make it through our goodbyes and our children's deployments again and again is to actually be aware of what we're doing and *how we feel when we're doing it*. I'm acutely aware of all my glowering in the wake of a goodbye, and the glowering doesn't actually feel that good. The chocolate tastes great, though. Maybe there's a way to skip the glowering and get right to the chocolate?

Maybe not, but it's worth considering. It's worth considering because I'm looking for every way possible to make our farewells a little bit easier on myself and on those around me. They will never be easy, I know. Not for us parents, and not for our kids—and certainly not for their kids, if they have them. Those farewells are the ones that break my heart into little pieces.

*M*ost military moms have seen a YouTube moment like this one: a pint-sized towhead is sitting in Circle Time as the teacher reads a story. Behind the boy, a uniformed stranger tiptoes into the classroom. Unsuspecting, the boy continues to listen attentively as his classmates' eyes widen. Realizing something is up, the boy swivels, then he leaps to his feet and jumps into his daddy's arms. And those of us watching at home on our computers are reduced to happy tears as the child clings to his father's neck, his body wracked with grateful sobs. "Daddy's home!"

These homecoming stories get me every time. And when my kids are deployed, they can turn me into Jell-O. *Just don't watch. Don't click on it*, I tell myself, but I can't seem to stop. From mommies rushing across football fields to daddies emerging from the waves in scuba gear for surprise reunions, I cannot get enough. Somehow, these homecomings feed my soul.

Funny how we never see videos of the goodbyes.

When our deployed children have children, our worries multiply exponentially. Not only do we worry about our kids, but we worry about our kids worrying about *their* kids. And naturally, we worry about their kids, too, and about our daughters- and sons-in-law. How will they handle being single parents for four or six or nine months? How will our grandchild or grandchildren adjust to their father's or mother's departure, absence, and return? How much do the children understand about what their parents are doing? How much are they worrying without letting on that they're worrying? Often it's hard to know, but sometimes the pain is right there on the surface.

A few years ago we received a frantic phone call from Tonya, Eric's wife. "Miles needs to talk to Poppa Courtney! As soon as possible!"

Miles—our eleven-year-old grandson—had just said goodbye, for the second time, to Eric, his stepfather of not much more than a year. The first goodbye had been one month after Tonya and Eric were married, and Eric's deployment lasted six months that time. Now, just five months later, Eric was deploying again. But this goodbye was different. Miles and Eric had become much closer, in spite of the challenge of Eric's lengthy absence. Miles was also a year older and had a deeper understanding of what the deployment could potentially mean for him and his mother—and, of course, for Eric. He was old enough to be frightened by the possibilities, just like his mother and I were. In fact, he was more than frightened; he was distraught, and Tonya wasn't sure how to handle it. She, after all, was also being torn apart by yet another separation in such a young marriage. So she did what we all do in the Brye family. She reached out to the calm, stable voice of reason. That would be Courtney, not me.

Courtney started right in as soon as our Skype call connected. "Miles, I know you are probably worried about Eric and feeling sad that he had to leave. You know he didn't want to leave, but it's his duty, right?"

Head nod.

"And you know that Eric is very well trained. In fact, he is one of the best pilots in the whole Marine Corps." (Parents are allowed to say that, right?) "Remember how Grandma Noni and I were in

Afghanistan? And how Aunt Katie was there? And remember how Uncle Jordan was flying over Libya? And how your great-grandpa was in a bunch of wars?"

Head nod.

"We all came back," Courtney said slowly and clearly. "Bryes come back."

And with that there was a glimmer of a smile on our grandson's face.

I am still not sure if that was the right thing to say. Making a promise like that is a risky thing. But at that moment, it felt right. It gave our grandson a measure of comfort and helped him get through the challenge of saying goodbye to someone he had come to love. And Eric came back, and he left again. That third time Miles seemed to have the emotional resources to handle it, or at least handle it better. At age twelve, he stepped up to be man of the house, and at this point, he is a seasoned veteran who has served in his own way.

Jordan's daughter was five months old when he left on his first deployment as a parent. The picture I have of him waiting to leave on the flightline with her in his arms gazing at daddy still brings me to tears. When he returned home, she didn't recognize him and wouldn't let him hold her for several days, which were several days of heartbreak for him.

All military families deal with tormenting situations like these. How do you explain to a two-year-old—or a two-month-old, or a seven-year-old—why mommy or daddy is gone? A Marine mom whose son is the father of two said to me, "The hardest part is how much it hurts him to leave his children. Each time he leaves, he knows they'll be different people when he gets back. He knows that he'll miss so much." And it's true; a birthday missed here, a holiday missed there—these things we can deal with. But when parents miss too many of the everyday moments—giving a baby her bath, tucking a little guy in, kicking a soccer ball in the backyard, helping with homework—on top of missing too many of the special days, that's not good for anyone.

My dad missed so much of our growing up. It was a hurt that stayed with him until he died. As a self-involved teenager, I couldn't see the enormity of his sacrifice; I was only concerned about how his absences affected me. I wish I could tell him now that I see those absences with different eyes, and that I understand the pull between service and self. I wish I could apologize for all the times I was spiteful or rude. I wish I could thank him for the legacy he created and the inspiration he gave to my children and my nephews and nieces. But in my childish world I did not see clearly. I struggled with being an Army brat, not realizing that he was struggling with disrupting us, and missing us, and at the same time doing whatever he could to protect his troops.

Now, as a parent, I understand how hard it must have been for him, so I try to be there for my children and grandchildren as much as possible. All military moms do. A mother named Denise told me that when her daughter deployed, she said to her son-in-law, "That's it. I'm moving in. If you don't mind, that is." She'd weighed the options and realized that it would easier for everyone if she were there to help with the kids. "And I knew it would make my daughter feel better, and that's all I cared about. I just wanted her to focus on doing her job and getting home."

Some deployments are easier than others when it comes to stepping in. "On the days I've received that phone call that my son was deploying within seventy-two hours to a destination he couldn't disclose, and a length of time that was uncertain, I was left with only two choices," my friend Judy told me. "Either lament and despair, or jump on the bandwagon and help him through what I knew was going to be a stressful situation. I've chosen to put on my military mom game face and say with a smile, 'How can I help?'"

What Judy's son seemed to need most from her was her reassurance that she would help look after his preschool daughter while he was gone. "And of course I said yes. My heart might be breaking, but you have to learn to keep your emotions in check. This is true of the first time he deployed, and still applies on the fifth or tenth time. It's never easy, but I try to focus on making it easier, not more difficult for him."

When we can't physically be there for our kids because of job responsibilities or financial limitations, or because we care for other family members, we may feel like we are being split into pieces. Teresa, an Air Force mom, did some creative problem solving and figured out a way to help maintain the ties between her son and his kids even though she lives far away. Every time she sends a care package to her son, she sends one to her grandkids, too. She makes sure to include things that will help them feel connected to their dad, like movies that he loved when he was a little boy, and pictures of him when he was their ages, and plenty of their favorite snacks—which just happen to be their father's favorite snacks, too.

When Nila, a Marine mom, learned that her son and daughter-in-law were expecting a new baby, and that it would be born while he was deployed, she immediately made plans to be on hand so that she could pitch in. "I'll be there to help with the other two grand-daughters," she told me. "Daddy can't be there, but at least he'll know I'm there to help take good care of all of his children, and that his wife isn't having to shoulder everything by herself. Anything to ease his mind so he can concentrate."

In Nila's words—and the words of Denise and Judy and Teresa and Nancy and all the other mothers who do what they can do help their children and grandchildren through the pain of being separated from those they love—I hear the momma grizzly bear strength shared by the Sisterhood of military moms. And I feel empowered by it. Your fortitude helps to boost my fortitude. We may worry, rightly so, about the impact that deployments have on our military kids and their families, but we won't stand by idly. When it comes to taking care of our cubs and *their* cubs, we find what works and we do it.

And what about us? We need care, too. So we keep evaluating our goodbye and deployment strategies to see what *really* serves us best, not just what we did last time. Maybe glowering works; maybe it doesn't. For me, chocolate works. I wish exercise did. I know knitting works. I know praying works. I know that doing things for my other kids works, and so do sending care packages and volunteering. And I know, beyond the shadow of a doubt, that holding the hands of my fellow military moms and feeling their strength and support— well, that always works, whether my children are deployed or right here in the land of the brave and the home of the free.

The Things We Carry

rendan has been selected for Army Air Assault School, and he has asked me to help him pack. For the tenth time, or so it seems, we are filling the giant green duffle bag with the items on the checklist. One packing misstep, one slight deviation from the packing list, and he'll be at risk of being sent home on the first day. Again and again he reviews the list and the items in front of us.

- Assault pack
- IBA/IOTV with name, rank, and plates (no side plates, yoke, groin protector, throat protector, or DAPS)
- ACH/Kevlar helmet (no cover)
- Waterproof bag, military issue (marked with shoe tag with name and unit)
- Wet weather top with rank (summer)/field jacket or Gor-Tex with all patches and tapes (winter)
- ACU top (sterile)

The list continues for three more pages; I hold up each item as he calls it out. Check, check, check.

"I sure *hope* you're wearing a helmet if you're rappelling out of a helicopter," I mutter. "And what's an assault pack anyway? That sounds dangerous."

I am rewarded with a steely gaze; Brendan doesn't like my half-hearted attempts to lighten the mood.

We finish the task, and the living room is finally cleared of the stacks of military paraphernalia. I stand in our driveway and watch his truck head south toward Fort Campbell, Kentucky. *Be safe*, I whisper. *Be safe.*

At the same time, another son is packing his large duffel in his own living room as he prepares to deploy.

Two children in harm's way: one in advanced training here in the states, and one far away on the front lines. This means that it's time for me to get my own essential gear together, just as my kids do, and man my own duty station. It's something that I do whenever one or more of my children is heading into a high-risk situation.

I know my packing list well. The items will go straight into my military mom backpack; I did a good job of making room for them years ago when I trained myself to eliminate some of the worry-bricks I had been carrying around. Fortunately, the survival aids I'm packing now don't take up a lot of space, and so there's plenty of room for them next to my knitting needles. But they are heavy, and I need my strength to carry them.

Like Brendan, I check the items time and time again. And while I'm doing so, I'm gratified to receive a stealth text from him. *I made it through the first day. 30 guys were sent home by noon.* And two weeks later, he receives his Air Assault Wings, one of 90 survivors out of 220 who embarked on the grueling course.

By then I have reported to my lonely battle station. I have guard duty, and it starts the moment any of my kids are in a potentially dangerous situation. I stay on post 24/7, and I'm always on high alert. I feel that in order to keep my children safe and our family intact, I have to be. Thank goodness I've got my survival gear with me.

ITEM ONE: LOCATOR BEACON
TO GUIDE YOUR LOVED ONE HOME

Home is where the Army sends you. That's the reality for servicemen and servicewomen, and it was certainly the case for me as a military child. Home to me was not a place, but having my family members with me. Six siblings, my mom, and sometimes my dad—that meant home no matter where we lived.

But what about us military mothers? We often *don't* have our family members with us. How is home where the Army sends you if you're not the one being sent? How is a home still a home if your children are hardly ever there?

My kids spent most of their childhoods on our little farm on the western end of the Appalachians. I have always likened the tiny nearby village to Brigadoon, the idyllic Scottish village that appears from the mists for only one day every hundred years. My Brigadoon, the one here in Ohio, has undulating hills and historic houses, and if you close your eyes, you can easily imagine life here a hundred years ago. Generations have grown up in this spot and never strayed far. It's a nice place to raise a family, tend a garden, and exist in peace. I didn't necessarily expect all of our kids to end up living close by as adults with their own families, but I did expect that the majority of us—a majority that would eventually include grandchildren!—would continue to celebrate holidays and important occasions together here.

Then duty called, and now my children are scattered to the wind. Every Thanksgiving, and Christmas, and Easter, I look around and see that almost all of the nearby houses have driveways overflowing with cars. It's a given that everyone comes home for the holidays. Not my kids. The needs of the Army, Navy, Air Force, and Marines supersede the needs of Momma. It doesn't matter that we mothers love our rituals and traditions and want to help pass them on to our grandchildren. The military can't afford to care that our kids miss weddings, reunions, and holidays.

In my Brigadoon, it's not the picturesque village that emerges so rarely from the mists and then disappears after the briefest of stays. It's my children. Courtney and I are here. Our farm is here. Our tiny town is here. But our children are not. I would be lying if I didn't confess to feeling the loss of them at holidays and family events as a sacrifice, and I'll admit that, yes, during one particularly lonely holiday season, I actually considered calling the local radio station and asking them to take "I'll Be Home for Christmas" off the playlist.

We military moms all have our lists of holidays and special events that our children have missed. A mom named Ann told me about her daughter's first Christmas deployed. "I always knew it was a possibility, and I didn't expect it to bother me so much, but when it happened I was a mess. And then I thought, *Get a grip, Ann. She's away from home with no tree and no one who really knows her. This is a lot harder on her than it is on me.* That really got me out of my funk."

Nila, a Marine mom, also gave voice to the gnawing anxiety and sadness that so many military moms feel during holiday season. "As Thanksgiving passed that year and we headed into the Christmas season, I could feel myself falling into despair. I didn't know if Jason would receive his Christmas box from us, or if he had even received his birthday box in October. It broke my heart to think of him in a foreign country without anything to open. But honestly, part of my sadness was for me. I just hated the idea of a holiday passing without hearing his voice." Exactly. We're sad for our kids and we're sad for ourselves.

Another Navy mom I know is also a Navy wife. With a husband in the military, she's had to celebrate many holidays and family events without him by her side. She thought she had the whole missing-special-events thing under control, but when her daughter had to miss her younger sister's high school graduation, "Well, I just wept," she said. Another mom shared with me the simultaneous sorrow and joy she will feel upon her youngest son's graduation from the Naval Academy. "His brother—his inspiration for attending the academy—cannot be there because he is deployed. I will spend the day rejoicing and grieving at the same time."

It is for all of these reasons that a Locator Beacon—a critical device for those who have lost their way, as it signals your location to search-and-rescue teams—is essential gear in any mother's duty station backpack. Our military children, deployed or not, are not able to be home much anymore; it is a disappointment all military mothers live with. And so we learn to keep our Locator Beacon activated and operating on its brightest setting so that our children can find their way back home to us when they're able to, and so that they can find us when we're patrolling the lonely emotional landscape out there on the perimeter of military parenthood.

ITEM TWO: BODY ARMOR

TO PROTECT YOUR HEART WHEN THEY ARE MISSING
LIFE'S BIGGEST EVENTS

When a child heads off for training or deployment, I do a quick personnel evaluation as I set off for my watch. Do we have any impending births? Are all family members stable? Do we have any elderly members who are starting to fail? To Do: Schedule FaceTime call with Grandma. To Consider: Do we tell her where he's going?

It hurts when our children miss holidays and special family occasions. We may feel their absences acutely, but we trust that there will be another Thanksgiving or birthday or anniversary to celebrate with them in the future. But when it's a birth or a death that our child must miss, the pain caused by his or her absence can be especially intense. That's when I don my body armor, hoping to deflect at least some of the incoming sorrow and grief. Body armor gives me the protection I need to keep from unraveling when I am pushed dangerously close to the edge of an internal precipice.

Sandy is a Navy Mom whose daughter and son-in-law were thrilled to be expecting their first child. A month or so before the birth, unexpected deployment orders arrived. "My son-in-law would not let his men go without him. The little guy was due two weeks after Daddy was supposed to leave, but lots of first babies come early, and so we all waited and counted down. But my grandson was not going to arrive fashionably early; he was happy where he was. And so Daddy said goodbye to his wife and unborn child and headed out."

Nothing seemed to go easily. The baby was a week late, and so Sandy's daughter was going to have to be induced. I speak from experience when I say that labor is hard enough, but kick-starting it with an induction is miserable. "The plan had been for me to go home and get a good night's sleep," Sandy told me. "But as her loneliness and the absence of her husband set in, my daughter said, 'I need you here.' I knew it wasn't me that she needed, it was her husband. But he was a warrior doing his duty, so she would do hers.

Through the night and on into the next day she labored on. He was able to get onto the phone and offer some encouragement, which she sorely needed. And finally, after thirty-six hours of labor, the baby arrived. Daddy could not see him—no Internet in his battle-front location—but we held the phone to the baby's ear and he could hear his daddy's voice."

I need you here. How many times have we thought this, or said this? And how many times have we wanted to say *she needs you here* as we watch a daughter or daughter-in-law struggle through labor and delivery and the care of a newborn? When a son or a son-in-law can't be present, though, we stand in as best we can, knowing all the while that we are no substitute.

When her son was deployed in Iraq, Judy's daughter-in-law gave birth, well before term, to a baby girl. "My son kept trying to call from overseas to follow the progress of the birth, but because of the time delay in the transmission, the maternity nurses at the hospital kept hanging up on him. After his daughter was born, I tried desperately to get a photo to send him but the nurses kept saying that only the father was allowed in the nursery. Explaining he was in a combat zone and was unable to actually be in the nursery, or even call, didn't seem to make a difference until I finally reached someone that comprehended the limitations of the situation."

Women give birth without their husbands present all the time, and not just because their husbands are in the military. This is nothing new. But when it's you giving birth without your partner, or your daughter-in-law giving birth very prematurely, or your daughter having an endless labor—well, the ache and the longing are profound. And the losses pile up. The first cry, the first smile, the first signs of an entirely unique personality—there are so many first moments that can never be recreated or shared.

And then there is the other end of the spectrum, when it's last moments that cannot be shared. As my father lay dying in hospice, we knew that our children could not be released to sit by his bedside. Eric was in TBS, The Basic School for Marine officer training, while Jordan was overseas training at the French Naval Academy. Brendan and Katrina were still in preliminary training and were in cell phone range, and they could speak to their grandfather even though he could not respond. I know it made them feel better; I trust that he heard them and understood, and that he felt better, too. Fortunately, the military moves heaven and earth to get loved ones home for funerals, so all of the kids were able to attend their grandfather's, but those final days without them by his side—and mine—were gut-wrenching.

My friend Pamela went through a similar difficult time when her son was in his second year at the Naval Academy. As she struggled every day to let go, bit by bit, of her son, her mother struggled with some serious health issues, and it became clear that soon Pamela would need to let go of her, too. Grandson and grandmother had always had a particularly close relationship, and it was hard for Pamela's mother not to have the one person who could always bring a smile to her face by her side at this difficult time. "My mother wanted Michael home but she wrote letters to support him to stay through the difficulties that he was facing himself. Her biggest fear was that she would die suddenly without him there. We both desperately missed him, but I knew that if either of us had said 'come back,' it would have killed his spirit."

Pamela's mother ultimately had a stroke as her beloved grandson was headed home on Christmas leave. Michael knew his grandmother hadn't been well, but he hadn't been aware of the severity of the situation, or of the stroke. Fortunately, the Navy parent who was giving him a ride home knew about the situation, and as they approached Michael's hometown, he explained everything to Michael and then delivered him directly to the hospital in uniform.

"When he entered the room, I was overjoyed to see him," Pamela shared. "He leaned over his grandmother, who lay connected to all kinds of machines, tubes, and wires, and he kissed her cheek and said 'Grandma, I'm here.' She opened her eyes and, for the first time, she smiled on the side of her face that was not paralyzed. Although she couldn't speak, her eyes so clearly said 'I love you.' Surprisingly, the nurse in the room addressed Michael as 'midshipman,' which is unusual outside of Annapolis—it turns out that she was prior Navy. She wished him luck and told him that his grandma had been waiting for him. To this day, I believe it was divine intervention that the Navy nurse was there to provide support to him at such a difficult time." Michael was able to spend the next few days with his grandmother before she died, and to be there for Pamela during a time of intense grief.

At some point, we will all live through times of pain and loss without our military loved ones at our sides. A difficult diagnosis, the death of a loved one, a grandparent slipping into dementia who will not remember her grandchild the next time he or she makes it home for a visit—the anguish of not having our military loved ones with us at times like these is one we will all share. And the anguish of not telling them the full extent of a painful situation or not being *able* to tell them (how do you reach someone on a submarine?) is a burden we also share.

I need you here. Yes, but our country needs them *there.* So even though relinquishing our children is a sorrow that runs deep, once again we must let go so they can do their duty. We continue to remind ourselves that their presence during life's monumental moments is a gift not a given. And as our sacrifices get bigger and bigger, we continue to armor up in an effort to protect our longing hearts.

ITEM THREE: COMM EQUIPMENT
TO KEEP DEEP CONNECTION ALIVE

The most difficult part of the perimeter guard's job is standing watch knowing that you will have little to no communication with the child you are waiting to hear from. That while you are vigilantly patrolling the perimeter, you are simultaneously losing connection with your son or daughter. This is why we need to have our communication equipment with us at all times. Our receivers will always be on. Always. Our children may only rarely transmit, but if and when they do, we will be ready to receive.

When your child is deployed, he may be half a world away—but who knows for sure? And if you don't know where your son is, you sure as hell don't have a clue as to what he's thinking or doing. Your daughter may touch base with you intermittently, usually in the form of a brief text or a Facebook message, but you probably won't hear her voice or have a real conversation with her for months. You will likely have no idea how she spends her days, no idea what she's worrying about or hoping for. You have no idea, because your deployed child cannot tell you. He or she might as well be on the dark side of the moon.

When a child is deployed or even in stateside training, we mothers sacrifice meaningful communication and by extension, and more consequentially, meaningful, deep *connection* with our sons and our daughters. And I often wonder if this loss of connection isn't ultimately one of the most painful and lasting outcomes of having a child in the military.

Sure, most children in the civilian world grow up and move away, they get married and establish separate lives. Communication diminishes. But with military sons and daughters, so much of their new life is required to be secret. They may be in dangerous places on difficult missions and be unable to tell us about any of it. When we don't know the things that are most important in their daily realities, the experiences that are shaping their futures for better or for worse, it becomes challenging, at best, to maintain the kind of relationship that we long for.

With each deployment, I have experienced losing touch with my overseas child—not just losing communication, but losing some degree of connection. I know that there's a good reason for it, and of course I will work to rebuild our connection when he or she returns. But I'm afraid that one day I may not be able to recapture the ground we've lost. I'm afraid that there will be things I can never understand because we can't talk about them, and if we don't talk about them, they will become barriers between us. I fear that one day I may lose a part of one or more of my children forever.

When my kids first joined the military, Courtney and I were by and large "due north," meaning that we were at the top of their emergency contact lists. But over the years, as my children have married and brought significant others into their lives, each of their compasses has shifted, and their own families are now due north. This is as it should be, of course. But for us mothers of married children, this means that we are no longer first in line for a conversation or a text when our child is able to make contact. Limited contact has just become all that much more limited. And if something bad were to happen—a thought that is hard to hold on to for more than even a moment—we will not be the first ones notified. In fact, my name—which appeared on birth certificates, countless field trip permission slips, report cards, and even the military enlistment paperwork at the recruiter's office—does not appear on any official notification list maintained by the military in reference to my married children. In the military's eyes, it's as if those of us who gave birth to these magnificent beings and helped prepare them to achieve what they're achieving today—well, we've been demoted to the ranks of the unimportant. It's almost as if we don't exist. Or at least that's how it feels sometimes.

That's a heavy weight to carry as I stand guard day in, day out. So I keep my equipment in perfect operating condition and remain ready to receive whatever precious morsel of communication that may find its way over the airwaves and through the wires and into my heart.

It All Takes a Toll

*W*hen a child is in the military, and especially when they're in an advanced training or deployed, military mothers operate in a heightened state of alert for an extended period of time. The strain takes a toll on us no matter how well we think we are holding up. After all, even the most well-trained warrior gets battle fatigued. And so do we.

Often the toll we pay takes the form of decreased emotional resilience or amplified emotional response. My friend Nancy shared a story that illustrates just how unstable and volatile our emotions can be when our kids are deployed. "It took less than a second for my eyes to flood with tears and my heart to go into overdrive. There, parked in my driveway, was a police car." With these words, I felt my own heart begin to race. "It was dark outside," Nancy continued, "and I was sure the police were waiting quietly for the Marines, who were on their way to notify us that something terrible had happened to my son, who was deployed in Iraq. Even now I have a hard time thinking about it.

"I told my daughter-in-law, who was visiting, and the two of us panicked. We waited and waited for the knock on the door, which didn't come and didn't come. But there the police car sat. When I couldn't hold my terror in any longer, I opened the front door and approached the car. That's when I saw the cop was taking a break and playing solitaire on his phone. I promptly lost it and began sobbing uncontrollably. The poor guy. He'd thought no one was home because all of the front lights were out. He felt so bad when he heard the circumstances."

An amplified emotional response, yes, and a completely natural one. To be a military mom is to be on high alert at all times, and false alarms are bound to be an occasional outcome of this constant strain. So is increased sensitivity to, oh, just about anything. Things that would normally roll off my back—a tone of voice that hits me the wrong way, for instance, or a careless remark—can leave me off balance. One military mom I know has told me that not reaching the phone on time when it rings can send her into a state of utter panic when her son is deployed—she's afraid of missing a call from him. The strain we're under causes other problems, too. Some of us don't sleep well. Some of us can't focus. Some of us use food or alcohol or something else to numb ourselves. Me, I love the temporarily calmness-inducing qualities of a nice piece of peanut butter toast.

Numbing ourselves isn't healthy, but sometimes it's so understandable. During a period of twenty days in January of 2014, there were five military aviation accidents with multiple fatalities. They included aircraft and helos involved in training and combat activities, and they took place at home and overseas. This relentless procession of tragedy was devastating to the relatively small community of aviator families; it would be almost impossible for anyone in this community not to have a connection to one of the missing, wounded, or dead. For my family, that connection was one of Jordan's classmates, the father of two young sons, who died in a helicopter crash off of the Virginia coast. As the search for the missing continued over several days and others fought for their lives, we all mourned. I can't begin to pretend to understand the deep wells of anguish and loss that those grieving spouses, children, and parents endured and must still endure. But as military parents we are connected in pride and sorrow. We grieve as a family when anything awful happens.

This sometimes means far too much grieving. As the wife of an aviator and the mother of three of them, I am no stranger to crashes and black smoke on the runway (my personal term for the deadly things that can happen in and around aircraft). Now, with the speed of news and social media, we might as well call it *black smoke on the Internet*. As soon as an accident is reported, the word spreads like wildfire. For a moment we are suspended as we calculate where the accident is, where our loved ones are, and what they might reasonably be doing. And then when we realize our kids are okay, we are flooded with gratitude and—shortly thereafter—guilt. Guilt that our children are still alive and another mother's son or daughter has fallen.

The technology that allows us to communicate instantly but also spreads bad news as fast as your Internet connection will allow is a double-edged sword. When our loved ones are deployed, we have so much more access to them than military families had in the past. But not hearing from our loved ones in this day of insta-communication can be just as anxiety-inducing as if we hadn't been hearing from them all along—or maybe even more so. As my friend Diana wrote in her journal during her daughter's deployment, "New Year's Day I was really crying. I had not heard from Janene for five days. How completely ridiculously my emotions were reacting! How incredibly spoiled I had become with modern communications. When my husband was deployed in the '70s I got one ham radio phone call in five months! And letters only occasionally—and now I'm worried sick because I can't get a text or e-mail from my girl? Yeah, yeah, I've repeated that to myself a million times, but until someone figures out a way to have one's intellect control one's emotions, nothing you rationally 'say' to your maternal self can talk you out of those primal feelings of love and fear and needing to protect your own."

Being able to know, almost in real time, about what is happening in your loved one's company or flight or squadron may seem like a good idea—until you stop to think of all the reasons why it's not. Can you imagine learning about the death of a loved one on Facebook? This was the real-life nightmare of a Navy wife whose husband's helicopter went missing when a huge wave washed it off the deck of an aircraft carrier in the Atlantic. She was officially notified when the helo went overboard, and she and her family and his shipmates held out hope he would be found and rescued. Several days after the accident, his body was located and a posting on the ship's Facebook page announced that he had not survived—before the casualty office made it to his wife's house to officially notify her of his death. My heart goes out to her and their children and his parents. In our darkest hour, shock and grief do not need to be compounded by the coldness of technology or the lack of human connection and compassion.

Sometimes we don't have enough information about our child's whereabouts to know whether or not we have any reason to be anxious, and then the waiting is interminable. "At the time of the Navy Yard shootings [in September of 2013], I had no reason to believe that my son was in harm's way, but I couldn't be sure, and I was aware of an underlying anxiety, even once I knew he was safe. As it turns out, unbeknownst to me, at the time of the shootings he was right next door at the Coast Guard facility," observed a military mother named

Celeste, a psychiatrist who works with the children of active-duty soldiers. So she was anxious when theoretically she had no reason to be, but actually she *did* have a reason to be. Which means, to me, that there's no rest for us, no true respite from the worry.

Our wild imaginings can be set off by the most innocent of triggers. A news story, a strange car in the driveway, or a ringing phone can send us into an anxious tailspin. And a missed call can send us down for the count. Ridiculous? Not logical? Doesn't matter. We are on adrenaline overload until our loved ones get home again. I don't know if anyone has ever done a health study on the impact of being a military mom, but I know that both the sustained stress and the moments of intense panic that we experience must take a toll on the body somewhere. At the very least, they explain the plethora of grey hairs I try to hide.

And when it all gets to be too much, I find myself seeking solace and calm in a simple, mechanical activity. Sometimes, when I want to create something from nothing, I knit. The clacking of the needles helps to bring me back to myself. Other times, I find all the pillowcases and handkerchiefs in the house, and I start to iron. The heat of the iron and the hiss of the steam take me straight back to age six, when I was practicing on pillowcases in order to win the honor of pressing my dad's fatigues. Not only is ironing mindless and productive, which can be a great combination in times of stress, but for me, it's an act of renewal: I can take a rumpled, crumpled mess and press it and press it until every wrinkle has been smoothed away and I'm left with something crisp and pristine and beautiful. It's almost like I'm giving it a fresh start. Which on some days, the days when having a child in the military seems to exact an impossibly high toll, is all I really want: a fresh start so that I can be there for my loved one, fully and completely, when he or she comes home.

The Sneaky Bastard

*W*e send whole, beautiful, perfect children to war. Some come home missing arms and legs. Others come home with invisible wounds that are the result of posttraumatic stress disorder (PTSD), traumatic brain injury (TBI), or more generalized emotional trauma. We are only beginning to understand the full repercussions of these forms of injury, but it is clear, as we look at the alarming numbers of soldier suicides and lives torn apart by substance abuse, violence, and emotional instability, that we need a war on brain injury and emotional trauma. We need to understand how to identify and treat those whose wounds are bloodless and whose scars are invisible.

"Without a doubt, the hardest moment for me as a military mom happened about ten years ago when one of my son's Naval Academy classmates came back from his deployment in the Middle East," a Marine mom once wrote to me. "He had been one of those good-natured, all around guys with service, faith, family, and community at his core. Seeing this young man who lit up the world with joy and laughter return from combat with hollow, expressionless eyes after losing some of the men that served under him simply broke my heart. He was no longer a carefree young man. In those few months since I had seen him, he had aged years. He didn't need to say a word. His blank eyes said it all."

She went on to speak of the death of another of her son's friends, a high school classmate. "Like so many of our war veterans, he committed suicide after his deployment. The demons that these young men and women face in combat linger long after they return. Their future is in our ability to identify and provide assistance for them. As a mother, I can't think of anything more important."

"Trauma is a sneaky bastard," observes Celeste, the psychiatrist, "and for those of us with kinfolk who are at risk, either as military or civilians—those in law enforcement, for example—there can be a slow, cumulative effect.

"How often do we think, 'How awful, how tragic' and 'Thank God mine are safe' all at the same time?" Celeste continued. "Each iteration of a fear-inducing incident and of that cycle—'Are they okay? Thank God they're okay'—serves to amplify our emotional response." So in other words, we mothers and fathers and family members don't become *de*sensitized to worry and fear, we become *more* sensitized to it every time the alarms go off. This has certainly been my experience, and I have to believe it's true for our veterans and those who have returned from difficult deployments. Trauma doesn't discriminate. It's a sneaky bastard for everyone.

Even without having been in combat myself, I have felt the sting of trauma's aftermath. When, on a serene and sunny day, my next door neighbor starts target practice in the middle of the afternoon, I have found myself on my living room floor more than once; I underestimated what a year of teaching in Kabul could do to one's reflexes. As upsetting as these episodes are, I understand that in the larger scheme of things they are pretty small potatoes.

Late in the afternoon of April 2, 2014, though, the residual effects of trauma's aftermath amplified all of my maternal instincts when news banners started to flicker across my iPhone screen about an active shooter at Fort Hood. *Why are they rerunning old headlines?* I wondered. *The Fort Hood shooting took place five years ago.* But underneath my puzzlement was a distinct sense of unease, so I ran to the living room to turn on my laptop and my television at the same time. As they slowly, too slowly, came to life, I texted a fellow military mom who is always on top of the news.

Just going to text you, she texted back.

So it was real: another shooting was in progress at Fort Hood at that very moment. At Fort Hood, where my youngest child was stationed.

I tried to remain calm. First I called Brendan. That's the quickest way to get in touch with him if he's able to pick up the phone. No response, but that's not unusual; he can't always pick up the phone. Texts, on the other hand, usually work. I texted. No response.

I looked up at the television, which had finally come to life. I almost wished it hadn't. A live video feed was playing, and I could hear the loudspeaker blaring through the housing area—ACTIVE SHOOTER . . . SHELTER IN PLACE—as well as the heart-rending sound of children crying. My anxiety ratcheted up several notches, and I closed my eyes for a few seconds to try to calm myself.

When I opened them, the banners across the bottom of the television screen seemed to be larger and more urgent than they had been just moments before. ACTIVE SHOOTER AT FT. HOOD, TEXAS ARMY BASE . . . MULTIPLE INJURIES. . . . My rational mind said, "There are thousands stationed there. It's a huge base. He's probably flying, so he can't be hurt." But my rational mind couldn't possibly talk me out of my fear, which was rapidly escalating as the news of the horror evolved on the television screen, and as the minutes ticked by without contact from him. And I couldn't help but fixate on the 2009 Fort Hood shootings that had left an incomprehensible thirteen dead and thirty wounded. I went into full-blown panic mode.

Answer the text, son. Answer!

I called Courtney, who was at work in Dallas, but all I could do was sob. "Shooting at Fort Hood. No word from Brendan," I finally managed to get out in a strangled voice. Courtney, always calm in crisis, tried to talk me down.

And then somehow the thought of those crying children just pushed me over the edge. *"But all those terrified little children are on lockdown!"* It reminded me of all of the times we practiced our lockdown procedures in Kabul in case the school was attacked. All of the times we led the children into safe rooms. All of the times we heard gunfire outside of the school compound. I started wailing again.

Finally, after an interminable fifteen or twenty minutes, a text from Brendan came in: "I'm OK." A moment later a second text came in, this one from his girlfriend: "He's OK." An hour later a third one came in, again from Brendan. "All my guys are okay, too." And isn't that the military way? Our men and women are trained to take care of each other.

But are we really doing all we can to take care of them?

When it was all over, it was clear that one soldier's mental illness had affected an entire community, and nation. The sneaky bastard had struck once again, and in its wake left a trail of tears and grief. I wept for the shooter's victims and their families. I grieved for the shooter's family. And I was angry—angry that he could not get the help he needed in time to prevent a catastrophe.

I want answers. I want treatment. This isn't the Civil War where we saw off legs and hope for the best. This is the twenty-first century.

PTSD, TBI, and depression are not signs of weakness. Gutting it out, embracing the suck, and using more willpower are not solutions for our veterans with these conditions. Just as we find new and increasingly sophisticated weapons to use in battle, we need to find new and increasingly sophisticated weapons to attack this issue—the soldiers we lose, though not to death—before anyone else gets hurt.

As of this writing, twenty-two US military veterans commit suicide every day. *Every day.* That's more than 8,000 a year, and because of inconsistent suicide-reporting mechanisms nationwide, and the difficulty of verifying the veteran status of the deceased homeless population, and the underreporting of suicide as a cause of death in general, it is believed that the actual number is far higher. Currently, the number of active-duty suicides is approximately 350 per year. It is estimated that at least 20 percent of Operation Iraqi Freedom and Operation Enduring Freedom veterans suffer from PTSD or depression or both, and 230,000 have been diagnosed with TBI. And news reports indicate that the Department of Veterans Affairs is woefully unprepared to handle the aftermath of this large-scale trauma.

As our sons and daughters re-acclimate to life at home, we worry that many Americans will forget that they may have invisible wounds. We grieve as we see strong young men and women crumble around us. We are horrified as we see some of them turn on their fellow brothers- and sisters-in-arms. And we are terrified for our own strong young men and women, who may be at risk simply by showing up to do their jobs on base.

But warrior mothers that we are, we are right in the middle of the fight for all of our wounded warriors, no matter how worried or frightened or exhausted we are. Injuries that would have resulted in death during previous wars are treatable, or more treatable, today. This means that there's a greater number of survivors than ever before, and a greater number of more seriously wounded survivors than ever before; some require months and years of extensive rehabilitation efforts. And it is the wounded warriors' family members—one million of them—who are stepping forward to take care of them.

There are some wonderful programs out there that offer support and encouragement to our handicapped veterans. We love it when we see houses built to accommodate physically impaired veterans and their families. We cheer for our para-athletes competing in all manner of sports. But when wounds are hidden, it can be harder to find help and even harder to know what to cheer for. Thank goodness for the efforts of Blue Star Families' Caregivers Empowering Caregivers (CEC) program. CEC offers workshops and materials that provide the resources, support, and tools that caregivers need to deal with both the visible and invisible wounds of war.

The demands of caring for someone with depression, PTSD, or TBI can be daunting. Susan, an Army mom whose son was injured by an IED in Afghanistan, writes, "I never envisioned giving up my job and moving away from home for a year to take care of my son. It just did not seem like a situation that I would ever find myself in. I had a friend whose son had a traumatic brain injury from a motorcycle accident, and I felt so sorry for her. I never dreamed that I would be dealing with these same kinds of issues. And I don't know what the future will bring."

The long-term impact of becoming a caregiver is something that most of us never thought about when our children made the decision to serve. But now that so many of us find ourselves in that position, we mothers need to fight, fiercely and tenaciously, for not only our extended family of military kids, but for our extended caregiving family. We need to advocate for increased funding for neurological research, suicide prevention, traumatic brain injury mapping, PTSD therapies, robotic limbs, technology innovation, and family caregiver leave initiatives. I appreciate the groundbreaking Joining Forces initiative that is supporting 130 medical schools and osteopathic colleges in training doctors to recognize and treat brain injuries, PTSD, and other mental health issues that affect our service members returning home from war. What else can we do? What else can everyone do? Our warriors, and their caregivers, deserve the best we have to offer both now and in the future, and we must do a better job of providing it to them.

I want to see an end to the violence that comes home from a war and sneaks up on you. Let's find the way to get rid of that bastard forever.

The Gold Star

A blue star that turns into a gold one. It's the transformation that every military mother and wife fears, and the one sacrifice that no amount of training or emotional toughening-up can ever prepare you for. It's the scenario that no parent or spouse ever wants to imagine, but that some of us can't help but contemplate on our darkest days. We hope and pray that our loved ones stay safe, but it's proven to us daily that there can be no guarantees. More than 6,600 times since the War on Terror began, a military mother or wife has donned a gold star.

When I meet a Gold Star Wife or Mom, my initial reaction is to panic. I don't want to say the wrong thing or do anything to open her wounds. I also feel guilty that my children are alive and walking around on this planet. And then there's the voice that whispers, "This could be you," which scares the heck out of me. But I also am overcome with sadness, and the sense of solidarity I feel with this fellow member of the Sisterhood usually outweighs my awkwardness. So most often, I reach in for a hug. And maybe I cry. Actually I always cry. Because her loss is my loss. It's everyone's loss.

I am always rewarded for pushing beyond my discomfort. I get to hear stories of amazing young men and women. And when I see the mothers or wives of those amazing young people standing in front of me, it gives me strength. I see that life does not end even in the presence of great pain. I see that those who have suffered unimaginable loss often find the grace to move forward with hope and courage.

Carmela is one of the many women who have suffered a mother's worst nightmare yet come through the darkness to offer light of her own.

I will never forget that day—September 16, 2004. The notification came shortly after four P.M. I had just picked up my youngest daughter and son from grade school. I think I must have screamed incredibly loudly because before I knew it, my neighbor was rushing over. I was only able to manage the words, "My son . . ." and he knew. He held onto me for what seemed like hours.

When I learned my Steven was going to Iraq, I knew his life would be cut short. I don't know how I knew, I just did. So when he was able to come home for a month prior to leaving, I made sure that he took care of personal matters, and I had to be in his presence constantly because I knew that he would not be coming back. When we said our goodbyes, I showed the brave face and expressed how proud I was of him. I kissed both of his cheeks and told him I loved him beyond measure. I didn't want to let go, but I knew he had to complete this journey.

On that fateful day, that day I found out, I became furious at God. How dare he take my child? And how dare he give me the "gift" of knowing about it before it ever happened? But as much as I was angry at God, it was in God that I sought my solace. Every morning I would call my pastor and ask him to please open the church. I spent hours there yelling, screaming, crying, praising, and praying, "Lord, please give me the strength to overcome."

I had two other children I needed to be strong for. Initially, in order to do what I had to do, I became like a robot. Then I started seeing a counselor; there were just too many questions I couldn't answer on my own. How can I be strong for my children? How can I continue with life when I hurt so much? How do I cope? How do I find a new normal? I was now a part of a group that I didn't ask to belong to. I felt like I had a tag on my forehead that said: "Look at me, I lost a child." Everywhere I turned there were words of encouragement, or condolences. All I wanted to do was hide away, but life wouldn't let me. As a single parent, I had to move forward. I had to get "it" together.

I don't recall the exact day, but it was probably two to three years after losing my son that I was walking along the waterfront alone. I was still in a foggy state of mind when an overwhelming sense of peace settled into me. It was then that I realized that yes, losing my child was painful and will always remain painful, however I was so thankful and so blessed to have had the privilege of being the one to give birth to such an amazing young man. I was blessed to have had him in my life for as long as I did. I was blessed for the lessons that he provided me in my own life. I was blessed for my other children to have been blessed with such an amazing and loving older brother. It was at that moment that I knew we were going to be okay, and that my son, while not here in the physical form, is with us every step we take. And he has let me know that he will not let go.

I would never want a Gold Star parent or spouse to feel burdened by being called a role model for resilience, or to feel like they have to live up to descriptions of themselves as "inspiring" or "indomitable" or anything else that makes them sound some way that they don't always *feel*. Sometimes having people tell you how strong and wonderful you are just isn't all that helpful. Still, it's hard not to use words like that about Carmela and all of the other Gold Star women who I've had the honor of meeting.

Lisa Hallet is another one of these women. I had the opportunity to get to know Lisa, a young Gold Star Wife, after I spoke at the Democratic National Convention in 2012. Lisa's husband, CPT John Hallett, was one of four soldiers in the 5–2 Stryker Brigade Combat Team killed by an improvised explosive device on August 25, 2009, while returning from a goodwill mission in southern Afghanistan. When he died, his and Lisa's third child, a daughter named Heidi, was just three weeks old.

When Heidi was born, John was in an area with very limited communications. Finally, when their daughter was five days old, Lisa got a call from him. "As usual during a deployment, there was a lot going on. We were refinancing the house, and there was so much to talk about—business details, logistics, the stuff of life. I was nursing the baby to keep her quiet, and John said, 'I haven't even heard her cry yet.' I thought, 'There will be plenty of time for that.' A few nights later I was giving baths to the brood, and I began crying. I had a three-year-old, a one-year-old, and a newborn, and it was just so hard to manage everything on my own. But I talked myself down. 'This is just a deployment,' I told myself. 'It's supposed to be hard. But he will come home and it will get better and life will be normal again.' Two weeks later, John was killed. He never did get to hear his baby daughter cry."

Looking back at my own mothering days, I remember the first month after each childbirth as a blur. I cannot imagine nursing a baby and taking care of other children and coming to grips with such a massive loss.

When I asked Lisa how she moved forward from a place of deep grief, she said, "My amazing friends stepped up to help me, and I never felt like an inconvenience. But I had moments that I wanted to be private. I didn't want anyone else to be the one to see that first smile. And all those other firsts, too. It was supposed to be John and me witnessing them.

"And I was not alone in my grief," she continued. "My military community lost forty-one soldiers, and we were all facing losses—if not of the life of a loved one, then of their limbs or minds. In the beginning it was a weird limbo, and then my friend said 'Let's run through this.' And we went for a run and the sun was shining and it felt so good. And then we gathered a few more friends, and we ran some more."

Those first runs led Lisa to cofound, along with Erin O'Connor, Alice Pope, and Sharlene Lewis, the organization *wear blue: run to remember*, a nationwide community of military members and their families, wounded warriors, Gold Star family members, and supportive civilians who run to honor the service and sacrifice of those in the military. Every week at different branches of the organization across the country, groups get together and run their hearts out in honor of husbands, wives, brothers, sisters, fathers, mothers, sons, daughters, company mates, and friends who have been lost but who live on in many hearts, as well as for those in the fight both on the battlefield and the home front.

I met Lisa when she contacted me to see if I could help find volunteers to hold flags next to posters displaying the faces of the fallen along the *wear blue* Memorial Mile of the 2013 Marine Corps Marathon. I did find some volunteers—a group of my moms from the Sisterhood. And I volunteered myself along with my daughter Katrina.

My experience on the Memorial Mile was agonizingly beautiful. Those of us who were there to help gathered early to remember the fallen. Standing in a circle, we called out the names of the honorees one by one. And then we spaced ourselves along one side of the mile-long memorial corridor, each of us holding a United States flag draped with a black ribbon displaying the name of our honoree. In front of us and alongside of us were the posters with the faces of the fallen. Most were smiling; all were too young. As the runners approached the wall of flags and posters, many slowed down and then were momentarily stopped in their tracks. Runner after runner brushed the images of the departed warriors with their fingertips and then slowly picked up pace again, touching each flag as they ran by. Every so often a runner would approach wearing the distinctive *wear blue* shirt; many had the name of their honoree scrawled on it. As the moms, the widows, and the loved ones of the fallen passed by, we could see them searching the posters for the faces of their departed ones. When they spotted the face they were looking for, an indescribable mix of grief and gratitude seemed to wash over them.

"It has been a difficult road," Lisa once told me, "but I'm fortunate that my life has been blessed by the inspiration of the past, the great potential of tomorrow, and the belief that the impossible is possible. It is up to me to harness the legacy." And it is by reminding herself of this, she said, that she keeps one foot moving in front of the other, day after day and mile after mile.

Moving forward, harnessing a legacy, honoring the fallen by supporting and inspiring the living—what acts of deep love and personal courage. I marvel at the fortitude of all of the Gold Star Wives and Mothers who forge their losses into service, whether service means caring for family, or community volunteerism, or founding a national organization—or nurturing a loved one's dream.

In the summer of 2013, I was answering the questions of the new plebe parents on the USNA-Parents listserv when I discovered that one of the plebe moms was already a Gold Star Mother. It was Carmela, the single mother of three who'd lost her son Steven in 2004. *How do you do that?* I wondered, incredulous. *How do you survive losing a son in Iraq and then have the strength to watch your second son take an oath to serve, too?* Carmela found the strength because she believed that her younger son, like his older brother, was doing what he was called to do.

Carmela told me that Bradley was five years old when Steven died. "Don't ever come to me and say you want to join the service," she said to him at the time. But later on in middle school, Bradley joined JROTC, much to her dismay. Previously he had been very shy, but with JROTC, he seemed to undergo a transformation; it was like he was doing what he was meant to do. Ultimately, he became the commander of his unit.

So she gulped and told him, "Okay, you can join the military as long as you don't join the Army or the Marines." When he responded that he wanted to join the military because it was the best way he could honor his brother, the Marine, and that his plan was to go to the Naval Academy and do the Marine option, she was speechless.

"And so I found myself watching him take that first step into Bancroft Hall, fully supporting him but finding it hard to breathe at the same time," Carmela said. "I love him and I never want him to feel like I am stopping him from doing what he is called to do.

"Today I don't dwell on the sadness or heartache of losing my older son," she says. "I rejoice that out of all of the millions of people,

I was chosen to bring such an amazing, awe-inspiring young man into this world. He brought so much love and so many lessons into our lives. He left this earth not only a hero, he left it having served a purpose, I am convinced of that.

"And every June 17, on his birthday, and every September 16, you will see me, and sometimes my children, letting go of balloons in remembrance of Steven. I don't visit his grave site. I don't believe he is there. I find him in the wind, on the radio, during my walks, conversations, laughter and tears, television, eating, around town. He remains in me forever."

I was struck by the serenity with which Carmela told the story of her journey through loss and beyond. I had been hesitant to ask her about it, but she had been eager to share. I see now that not only was hearing her story a gift for me, but that telling it was a way for her to honor her son.

And I would like to say to all Gold Star parents and families what I said to Carmela: you are not alone. You are part of a large extended family that holds you close with loving arms. I cannot pretend to know the full experience of your loss and your anguish, but I can promise to do my best to honor your sacrifices and keep your loved ones' memories alive. On Veterans Day, Memorial Day, and when I visit my dad at Arlington National Cemetery; when I see an American flag, hug my grandchildren, or feel the wind on my face, I will remember you and the ones who live in your hearts.

No Guts,
No Glory

No Guts, No Glory

*B*OOM!

The cannon thunders into the warm October air and off we go. Eighteen thousand runners—and me. *What have I gotten myself into?* I wonder for the hundredth—no, thousandth, hell, the ten thousandth—time since I'd put my name into the lottery for a slot in the Marine Corps Marathon earlier that year. I'd done it on a whim—a well-intentioned but ill-conceived whim—when Jordan had been accepted into the Naval Academy, and I'd figured that as he was enduring his long hot Plebe Summer and pushing himself to his physical limits, I might as well do the same. I told no one but Eric about this crazy idea; he was a runner and competed on the Navy track team (though no one imagines for a moment that he inherited his track talents from me; those all came splashing from his father's gene pool). And oh, by the way, have I mentioned that I hate running? And that I was completely out of shape? I thought: *Just because I put my name into the lottery doesn't necessarily mean I'll win the slot and actually have to go through with it, right?*

Of course I won a slot.

I knew I couldn't back down, and so as Jordan grunted his way through Plebe Summer, I lumbered down our local trail, crying, praying, and wondering what spark of insanity had possessed me to put my name into that damned lottery. I channeled all of my worrying about Jordan into my own training, and came to see each painful step, each arduous mile, as way to align myself with all the miseries that he would be enduring that summer. He had no idea then that I was identifying and commiserating in a very real way with the way he was being pushed physically, but I knew it. It was an act of solidarity.

I tried to remind myself of these nobler goals when I found myself on the starting line that October sporting my *Navy Mom* T-shirt and near hysterics. *What have I gotten myself into?* The gun went off, and I was swept along in a sea of runners. I was with those who averaged a mile in fourteen minutes "plus" (what a polite way of saying it), but even so, that pack began to thin as some runners pulled ahead and others (ahem) remained slow and steady. I knew I was in trouble when, sometime early in the race, I was passed by a man who appeared to be over a hundred years old, and then, not much later, by a one-legged runner. But I kept going. During most of the race one or more of my kids showed *their* solidarity and jogged beside me as I shuffled along. Because he was a plebe, Jordan was required to be in his service dress blues uniform—long pants and a snappy double-breasted blazer, tie, and white shirt—any time he was off base. So he ran alongside me in full uniform, cover included. He didn't have to worry about breaking a sweat, though. I was moving slowly enough that he just had to slightly extend his long legs to keep pace with me as I plodded on.

I finished that 26.2-mile gauntlet completely and utterly miserable and jubilant at the same time. My *Not Last* plaque tells the whole story: I wasn't. I was sixtieth from the rear out of those eighteen thousand plus runners, and my plaque sits in a place of pride on my bookshelf. It reminds me, on a regular basis, of that one-step-at-a-time approach I have used over and over again. One step at a time to make my way through difficult hours, days, weeks, and months; one step at a time to transfer worry into forward movement; one step at a time to accomplish the apparently impossible. Yes, I was utterly miserable physically upon completing the grueling race, but my jubilation far outweighed my body's aches and pains. I had set a laughably out-of-reach goal for myself, a goal that I would have to try to achieve in front of more than eighteen thousand other people, *and I had achieved it.*

No guts, no glory.

When I think of setting a ridiculously difficult goal and then doing whatever it takes to achieve it, I can't help but think of my good friend Joy. A few years ago, this fifty-nine-year-old wonder woman of a mom participated in a boot camp experience purchased for her by her Navy daughter. That experience inspired her to train for a Spartan Race, a push-your-limits, test-your-strength, challenge-your-endurance combination of extreme obstacle course and run. I clicked on the YouTube link she sent me for her race, and my jaw dropped. Up and over the wall, through the concertina wire, across the muddy ravine—over and under the obstacles she flew, reaching, grabbing, leaning, crawling through the mud. Whatever it took to complete the race, she did.

Is there a more apt metaphor for what we do as military moms? No matter what comes our way, we lean in to meet the obstacle, whether it's a child at sea who's unable to communicate for months at a time, or one with boots on the ground in an unknown location in hostile territory, or one on rapid deployment pace with no let-up in sight. We are in an endurance race that is seemingly never-ending, and we do what we need to do to support our kids and to finish the race ourselves. They are on a course that we cannot alter, and we are right there beside them in our hearts and our minds. They need guts in order to achieve their goals, and we need guts in order to overcome the challenges their choices present to us.

No guts, no glory. It's not just a buzzy motivational catch-phrase. It's a way of life, one that we military moms live and breathe every single day.

It's been fourteen years since I accompanied my firstborn to the Naval Academy and watched him ascend the stairs of Bancroft Hall, beginning his journey away from home and toward his destiny. In short order, the rest of the brood followed suit, each in his or her own way. When Courtney and I were finally alone in our empty nest, I thought I would feel isolated—Courtney is so frequently away—and overwhelmed with worry and anxiety as my children flew into harm's away. Imagine my surprise to find instead that I am the farthest thing possible from isolated. I have embarked on my own journey, and my path as a military mom has been full of unexpected blessings. Chief among these blessings are my relationships with my fellow mothers in the Sisterhood, relationships that enrich my life every day. Over the years, as I have learned their stories and the stories of their amazing children, these Sisters and their kids have become the wind beneath my wings, buoying my soul and giving me hope for the future.

How could I not be inspired by the story of the single mom who pinched pennies and took the megabus halfway across the country so she could attend her son's boot camp graduation because, as she says, "no one in our family has ever accomplished something like this before. I want him to know how proud we are that he is standing up for something important. That he is worth riding a bus for eighteen hours in order to see him graduate."

Without the guts to scrimp and save and ride the bus all that way, she'd lose the glory of seeing him graduate.

How could I not feel solidarity with Miranda, whose son swam against the tide of popular opinion to follow his calling? She is a self-described Foreign Service brat who comes from a long line of Yale graduates, and her family lived overseas for two decades—protected, always, by the Marine security guards. But when she was at Yale, she swiftly learned that defending the US military was not going to make her any friends; ROTC was not even allowed on the campus. The same was true at the elite law school she attended. Still, when she moved with her young family to a very highly educated, wealthy liberal community in the Northeast, she was shocked by the low regard spared for our troops.

When it came time for her son to choose a college, he made it clear that he was not interested in attending her alma mater, or any other Ivy League school for that matter. "Ivy League friends and acquaintances were aghast when he accepted his appointment to the Naval Academy," Miranda told me. "They said remarkably harsh and ignorant things, like 'Why would you ever let your son waste his life with a bunch of followers?' and 'People only join the military if they have no other options' and 'He's joining the Navy? You must be so disappointed that he's not going to college.'"

As Miranda told me this story, I could feel my blood start to boil. But I didn't need to give voice to my anger; she did it for me. "How could we live so long in this bubble surrounded by such ungrateful people? Everything they have, everything they enjoy, has been bought by the blood of young men and women like my son who are willing to stand for freedom, for democracy, and for the right for them to say and do what they want."

No guts, no glory. Miranda's son lives this every day, and she does too.

Over and over, I see the strength of character of so many unheralded military parents. The mothers and fathers who stand by their injured sons and daughters, some of whom may never totally recover, leave me both humbled and inspired. I salute the efforts of so many mothers and wives to honor and remember the sacrifices of those gone before. The founders of organizations like the Matthew Freeman Project, which, as part of its support for grieving family members, makes teddy bears out of fallen family members' uniforms; and the Travis Manion Foundation, whose mission is to assist our nation's veterans and the families of fallen heroes; and *wear blue: run to remember*, which acts as a support network for active-duty service members, veterans, and both Blue Star and Gold Star families, have taken anguish and grief and transformed them into service and aid for others. I think of Carmela, the Gold Star Mother who stands by her younger son as he prepares to follow his fallen older brother into harm's way, and her strength and composure help me when I need to summon those qualities in myself.

And then there are the warriors themselves. Many of those who serve have shown both quiet courage and fierce determination on their paths to service. Like the plebe so terribly injured during her Plebe Summer at the Naval Academy that she spent her entire plebe year in a wheelchair. Multiple surgeries would have caused someone with a fainter heart to throw in the towel, but even as healthy plebes around her dropped out, she remained resolute. And her mom stood alongside her, backing her decision to stay every inch of the way. Now that fiercely determined young woman is an accomplished

Surface Warfare Officer. Her battles were fought early under circumstances that would have caused most people to quit, but she gutted it out.

No guts, no glory.

And there's Will. When I first saw pictures of him with Jordan and Jordan's company mates during their Plebe Summer, I wondered, "Who is that old guy? And what's he doing dressed like a plebe?"

It turned out that he was a twenty-three-year-old prior Marine, and he was Jordan's roommate. And yes, he was, in fact, a plebe. Every year there are a number of enlisted sailors and Marines selected to attend the Naval Academy for officer training, and this particular year, Will was one of them. He had already been deployed to Germany, had served at 29 Palms, and was a graduate of the school of hard knocks. He was five years and a lifetime of experience older than the rest of his classmates.

Over time—Will and Jordan ended up rooming together all four years at Annapolis—I slowly learned more about the independent young man. Will had moved out from a difficult family situation when he was sixteen years old, and as soon as possible, he enlisted in the Marine Corps, where he made the best of his opportunities. After five years, he applied to and was ultimately was accepted into the Naval Academy. He was a completely self-made man and quickly became a resource for his much younger company mates. Have a financial question? Ask Will. Need some wisdom on leadership and working with enlisted Marines or sailors? Ask Will. Need help navigating the chain of command? Ask Will.

The better I got to know Will, the more I marveled at his accomplishments and his maturity. When I tried to imagine what his life had been like before he left home, I wondered if it had resembled those of some of the at-risk students I taught in high school. I wondered if his home situation had been anything like that of Jesse, one of my students who lacked focus and had a reputation for trouble. Jesse was taking my sophomore biology course as a senior; he'd already taken it once and failed it. As the year wore on, I tried to encourage Jesse, as I encouraged all of my students, but he struggled to stay on track, and more than once I thought all was lost. After he graduated I heard he'd enlisted in the Marine Corps. I was glad and worried at the same time. Would he be able to make it, or would the demanding experience be just one more crushing blow to his ego?

Fast-forward several years. My daughter was visiting my classroom giving a speech about the Naval Academy when three strapping young Marines knocked and entered. *Why are these recruiters visiting my class?* I wondered. No sooner had I asked myself the question than I was enveloped in a giant bear hug. When I got a good look at the uniformed man giving me the hug, I realized it was Jesse. He had come to pay a visit with two of his high school classmates who had also enlisted and were now serving their country.

Jesse released me and grinned. Then my daughter, amazed, walked over, and the three snapped to attention.

"Good morning, ma'am," they chimed in unison. Four years prior they had all been students in the same high school. Now she was an officer charged with the responsibility of leading troops. The respect they showed her was almost palpable, and I saw in action the results of their transformation. So I did what any mom and teacher would do—I ran to find the Kleenex.

Jesse and his buddies are Afghan War veterans. Will is married and has a great job after a stint as an Information Warfare Officer in the Navy. Their valor is of a quiet nature, but exceptional all the same, and their stories are replicated over and over again on the ground, on the water, and in the air.

Strength developed through adversity. Guts into glory.

*I*t's graduation day at Naval Amphibious Base Coronado in Coronado, California, home of the Basic Underwater Demolition/ SEAL (BUD/S) training facility at the Naval Warfare Center. On one wall of a simple beachside structure there's a sign that reads *The Only Easy Day Was Yesterday;* another sign on another wall reads *Be Someone Special.* Normally NAB Coronado is the site of all kinds of advanced physical training, but today those on base are focused on one thing only: the graduation of forty new Navy SEALS—clearly *Special Someones*—who are about to receive their SEAL pins. It has been more than two years of arduous training for these future Special Forces warriors, and the helmets lining the compound give silent testimony to those who did not complete the grueling course; there are many more helmets than graduates. Also there is the bell where a candidate goes to "ring out" if he decides to quit. And there are many reasons to quit. Injuries, and mental, emotional, and physical strains—they all take a toll. The men who "rang out" here at NAB Coronado were brave enough to try. There is honor in that.

But the focus today is not on those who came short. It is on those who will celebrate a significant milestone along the path to their dreams. The reality is that their work is just beginning. All told, they will go through approximately three years of advanced training, and then they will sink into the silent world of active-duty special operations. That is in the future, but at this moment I am here to witness the success of one special young man.

I came to know him and his parents during Katrina's Plebe Summer, when she developed a whole new group of brothers within 4th Company; those strong friendships remain intact to this day. One of Katrina's best buddies was Greg, whose mother, Sherry, I had quickly hit it off with on the USNA-Parents listserv. Like Katrina, Greg was also an aeronautical engineering major, so he, Katrina, and another company mate, Travis, formed a study group and spent hours working on projects together. Katrina and Travis wanted to fly, but Greg had his mind set on becoming a SEAL. He dedicated all his efforts with a laser beam focus to that goal, spending every free moment working out in the gym and the pool. He received accolades and increasing positions of responsibility. The stars were aligning, and it seemed like he was on track to reach his goal.

In November of Greg's and Katrina's senior year, though, when service community assignments were announced, Greg learned that while another company mate was SEAL-selected, he had been assigned to Surface Warfare. The average man would have given up. Not one with the warrior spirit.

After taking some time to reorganize, Greg returned to training with a new vigor. Despite being assigned to a ship and having a job with intense demands on his time, he continued to push himself to be his best physically, mentally, and professionally. Two years after graduation from the Naval Academy, he was selected for BUD/S training, and for the next two years he worked through the series of rigorous trainings that are required to become a SEAL. Finally, after several setbacks that jeopardized his ability to complete the training, he was here, triumphant, at the finish line.

No guts, no glory.

Jubilation and excitement provided a thin coating over the terror in this mother's heart as I reflected on what Greg might be called to do somewhere down the line. And this is the crux of the matter: for those of us whose children have chosen the difficult path of defending our nation and preserving its freedom, an irresolvable tension exists between fear on the one hand and pride and happiness on the other. But warrior parents that we are, we allow our pride in our children's characters and their desire to make a difference in the world lead us to choose happiness at times like these.

There is the bravery required to go out and fight the battles, and there is the bravery to keep the home fires burning. Each is an act of heroism. In my mind, all of the parents who grin through their tears as their sons and daughters prepare to go out and do very difficult things in the name of freedom are heroes.

*A*fter so many years of enduring separations from loved ones— my entire lifetime, in fact—and so many sacrifices and sorrows, how can I take my place in the ranks of military moms with a smile on my face? It's quite simple, really. It's all about love.

I love my country. It is a place like no other on earth. I say this having had firsthand experience living under a veil of darkness in a country where, because I am a woman, my life and liberties were ranked second-class, or worse. I have seen the ravages of war, and poverty, and communism. I will never forget taking the train as a teenager and crossing the border from West Germany into East Germany on our way to West Berlin. Dramatically, in literally a second, the scenery changed from glorious Technicolor to somber black-and-white.

The United States is not without its flaws, yet our quality of life as Americans is still something for which I thank my lucky stars every single day. My children can go to school without paying or walking miles to get there. My daughter is not harassed or killed for trying to get an education. We can all vote and have confidence that our votes count. We can trust our military to work in concert with our government rather than undermining it. We do not fear military coups or live threatened by corrupt police.

And all of this is possible because in every generation we have a group of young people who feel called to serve, to protect and defend our constitution and all that it promises us. A group of young people who are willing to leave the comforts of home and risk life and limb to protect us and all we hold dear. I am grateful to each and every one of them. What a glorious thing.

I look at my own children—those babies I carried and nurtured so carefully who have now gone out into the world in our country's service. I hold my breath as they soar into the sky or don their battle gear. I marvel at them and their band of brothers and sisters who are willing to risk all for us. I pray—oh yes, Lord, I pray—that they continue to come home. And I also marvel at all they have become. To watch a rocket that Katrina helped launch stream into space; to see a mighty Chinook helicopter climb into the sky carrying much-needed equipment with Brendan at the helm; to know that Jordan's reconnaissance flights helped provide aid and assistance to survivors of the devastating earthquake in Haiti in 2010; to watch as Eric races down the runway and takes off in his F/A-18 in a stupendous ball of fire—these things make my heart swell. And when, in my mind's eye, I see the image of my oldest son lifting off in his supersonic aircraft, I can't help but remember the dreams of a little boy who longed to be Top Gun, and the roaring blaze of the afterburners streaming heavenward seems to me a glorious metaphor for the way every single one of our children who has the guts to serve soars to his destiny.

I frequently travel across the country. As I look down from thirty thousand feet, I often think about my fellow members of the Sisterhood who are scattered across our great nation and beyond. Some of our members had never set foot on a military base before their son or daughter announced, "Mom, I want to join the military." And with lumps in their throats, those mothers went with their children to the recruiter to sign the paperwork, wondering what in the world the future held in store for them and their families. Other moms, those living on bases, had packed up and moved dozens of times as their husbands or fathers performed their duties in the service of their country. Still other moms had served themselves and knew intimately the challenges and rewards that their child would face. No matter where a military mother falls on the spectrum, each is a momma who has given her most precious gift to her country. And each momma has signed up for an extended tour as Watch Stander on the Home Front Command Post.

We stand watch on our post night after night, day after day, because of the overwhelming pride we feel knowing that it is *our* children who carry the banner of freedom; this is what helps us endure all those sleepless nights. We fight back all our worries and fears because we love our country. We love our country enough to give our children up. We love this nation and its principles enough to stand and say, "Take my precious child and make him or her a warrior."

We know that our sons and daughters are worthy of our respect and gratitude, and we accept they have been called to fight for freedom. We know what it took to get them to where they are today—the bravery, the stamina, the sacrifices, the guts. We raised them. We had a front row seat.

So here's to all the unsung heroes—those mommas who have had the guts to let go, toughen up, remain *Semper Gumby*, embrace the suck, and carry on.

I am proud to serve with you.

Acknowledgments

$\mathcal{I}$t takes a village to produce a book, and we would like to thank the entire extended PublicAffairs village that has brought this book into being, starting with Peter Osnos, founder and editor-at-large. Thank you, Peter, for seeing the possibilities of this project and for introducing Nan into the mix. Thank you to publisher Clive Priddle for taking a chance on it and affording us the privilege of reaching out to so many military moms.

Our editor, Emily Lavelle, must have been a drill sergeant in another life. Her passion and savvy and commitment to this book helped us polish these stories till they shone, and her manifold contributions have made the book better in every way. We would not be where we are without you, Emily, and we appreciate all of your suggestions, even the ones that hurt!

The production team has been a pure pleasure to work with, starting with managing editor Melissa Raymond, who has shepherded the book, and us, through the production process with efficiency and grace. Thank you to Deborah Heimann, our copy editor, for making us look our best and for her kind words; to our text designer, Pauline Brown, for finding a way to replicate the tone of the book with her visual choices; and to our proofer, Rachel Shirk, for her keen eye. And a huge, heartfelt thank you to Pete Garceau, the jacket designer, for hitting just the right note. We are grateful to you every time we pick up a copy of the book. (And how did you know to feature a flightline with a waiting C-130, the exact aircraft, down to the model, that Courtney flew in Vietnam? The image evokes memories of so many tearful goodbyes and welcome homecomings.)

Gratitude to Lisa Kaufman, marketing director, for her expertise and expansive thinking, and for valuing the book in a personal way; and thanks to her entire staff, especially Lindsay Fradkoff, social media maven. Jaime Leifer, publicity director, and Jill Siegel, of Jill Siegel Public Relations, have worked overtime to bring the book to the attention of readers both military and nonmilitary, and we are grateful to them for everything they have done. And of course we appreciate the efforts of Matty Goldberg, Perseus Books Group president of publishing, client sales and development, and of the wonderful Perseus Books Group sales team, as well.

ELAINE LOWRY BRYE

In addition to the team at PublicAffairs, there are so many others who have cheered us on and contributed to this book. It is my pleasure and privilege to acknowledge:

The countless members of the USNA-Plebe-Parent listserv, the USNA-Parent listserv, the USNA Parent Community Facebook page, and the USNA Class of 2016, 2017, and 2018 Mom and Dad Facebook pages who urged me to write a book someday; my fellow moderators and administrators on those pages who supported me as we supported Navy parents; Barbara Craig, who not only served as a moderator but also supported many families in serious medical situations including my own; West-Point.Org for hosting and the Naval Academy Alumni Association for partnering with the USNA-Parents listserv and providing a place where Navy parents could communicate.

Linda Brinson, USNA Class of 2010 mom, English professor, and editor who encouraged me to sit down and actually write the memoir that was the genesis of this book.

Steve and Katie Scully, USNA parents, who gave me guidance and encouraged me to send the initial manuscript onward. The result is an actual book!

Nan Gatewood Satter, my coauthor, who has earned her star as an honorary Blue Star Mom. During the time we wrote this book she has endured with me deployments, aviation fatalities in the families of my friends, and the death of one of my colleagues in Afghanistan. She has truly walked in my shoes as a military mom, and I have watched her compassionate heart break. I have appreciated her steady hand and attention to detail as I have gone through the agonizing process of pushing back the curtain that we military folks are trained to hide behind so that I can tell the real stories. Thank you for your guidance, your excellence, your support, and most of all your friendship. I could not have done it without you.

My dearest fellow members of the Sisterhood, who came forward and shared their stories so generously and willingly in order to ease the burdens of other military moms. Most of these mothers and Sisters would be glad to disclose their names, but for the sakes of their children, we decided it was best to keep their identities private. Ladies, I treasure each and every one of you. You are the greatest assets a military mom could ever have, and I cannot imagine the last fourteen years without you. Thank you for your many, many contributions. You know who you are in this book, even if your kids don't. Here you are by pseudonym—enjoy your alter egos! Lynn, June, Melinda, Tina, Regina, Georgia, Dana P., Melissa, Julie, Anita, Samantha, Sandra, Janet, Shirley, Lisa, Connie, Dana S., Caroline, Mary, Gina, Karla, Clarissa, Sandy, Maria, Mike, Jana, Amy, Sheila, Vickie, Nancy, Denise, Judy, Teresa, Nila,

Lurline, Juanita, Ann, Sandy, Pamela, Diana, Celeste, Susan, Carmela, Jill, Miranda, and Sherry.

Gold Star family members Carmela and Lisa Hallet, my heartfelt thanks and special blessings for discussing such difficult memories. We all will hold your loved ones in our hearts and never forget.

Will, my "adopted" son—I am so proud of the man you have become.

Sheila Stevens, vice president of Blue Star Families, for all the work you do, especially when I call you with a family in need. You are appreciated.

First Lady Michelle Obama and Tina Tchen, the first lady's chief of staff. When you responded to my Christmas card with a dinner invitation, it was more than just a dinner invitation. It was an affirmation that a military mom from a farm in Ohio mattered because her kids were important. That was an empowering, life-changing message, and I continue to carry it with me everywhere I go. It's one of the reasons I wanted to write this book. Our military children are exceptional, and deserving of our deepest gratitude, and who better to remind America of that than the Mom-in-Chief. Thank you for caring about our military kids.

Dr. Jill Biden. As a military mother, you know firsthand just how hard this life is. Thank you for everything you do to support all military families.

My special group of hometown friends—especially Diane Dailey Gardner and MaryAnn Prosko, also a military mom—who have gathered around my family and me for the past thirty years, and who have supported me as my role changed from Winona farm wife to that of military mom. You have always been there encouraging me even when the journey took us off the beaten path.

The dear friends who shared my Afghanistan experience—some of whom were physically there with me, including Allie Harrington,

Amanda Earnest, Heidi Miller, and Jan Schuitema—and some of whom were there in spirit. Thank you Susan Seligman, Joy Krebs, Jane DeHart, and Holli Hamner for your support and willingness to listen to the stories even when they were hard to hear at times.

Allie "Miss Brill" Harrington—for the photojournal of our time together "in country" and the photo for the back cover of the book.

The best sponsor parents in the whole world, Dede and Randy Brown, USNA Class of 1957.

My battle buddies Nita Reddinger, Diane Peske, Signe Donaldson, Marisel Morales, Monica Ellington, and Jan Schull, who have shared deployments, care package recipes, late night phone calls, and panic attacks, not to mention prayer requests. We have cried together when our children have deployed and cried together when they have returned. Where would I be without you?

My sisters and brothers—Susan, Jane, Michael, Kathleen, Mary, and Phillip, Jr. We traveled all over the world together, like barnacles attached to our mom, as our dad zipped in and out of our lives, and despite the wounds we bore and the sacrifices we made, we are one amazing family. Mom and Dad left us an amazing legacy. I am proud to be an Army brat. I am proud to be a Lowry.

My nephew Luke. You came into the family with a whirlwind of energy and there was no looking back. I have purposely kept your story private so that you can make your own choices, but I want you to know that your commitment to rugby is scarier to me than any military training so far. (I'm not entirely kidding.) Courtney and your cousins and I love and respect you. And don't worry. I didn't tell that story about you climbing to the top of the ladder in the barn when you were three and telling me you weren't afraid of nothin'. I have confidence that with that attitude you can do anything.

My children, Eric, Jordan, Katrina, and Brendan. Unlike the children of other mothers in this book, you do not have the luxury of flying below the radar. Sorry about that, but you're stuck. For years you bore the burden of waiting until I could respond to a hurting parent's e-mail or having dinner be late because I was on the phone. And now maybe someone will recognize you, and you might have a little extra attention because of this book; I apologize for that in advance. But you also know that there have been countless parents who have been grateful for whatever I could offer them, so you have graciously put up with sharing me. You have even done what you could to help when I needed information or perspective that you could provide. I cannot express how much I appreciate your willingness to support me with this "ministry" to other parents. I know your natures are to stay out of the limelight, so sacrificing your privacy is all the more appreciated. I love you all forever and always. Thank you for being who you are and for the choices you have made for your country. I am so very proud of you all.

My daughters-in-law, Angela and Tonya, and son-in-law, Preston, for standing by my kids. Thank you for holding down the fort during multiple difficult deployments, sharing phone calls and messages from your spouses, and supporting me throughout the writing of this book. A special thanks to Tonya, who took my wonderful author's photo and others as needed—what a gift you have for making people look good. Thank you Miles, for stepping up to be the man of the house. Angela, thanks for taking such good care of the babies when Daddy is gone and taking care of so, so many others at the same time. And Preston, United States Air Force Academy 2009 and USAF Huey pilot, thank you for your service; you make us proud.

My husband Courtney. Thank you for being the rock (as usual) through the panic attacks when I thought there was no way I could ever write a book, and the times when it seemed like I had nothing worthwhile to say. You are a constant positive force in my life. Thank you for your encouragement and for helping me take it one step, one page at a time, like you have been doing for thirty-seven years.

The children who grow up and decide to serve, and the moms (and dads) who let them: our nation owes you all a debt of thanks. Add mine to the list, for where would we be without you?

Be safe.

Love, Momma Brye

NAN GATEWOOD SATTER

Elaine Brye is the partner everyone dreams of. What a gift to work with someone whose dedication never wavers, and whose work ethic can only be described as, well, military. Thank you for welcoming me into your family and your world, and bringing every bit of your courage, wisdom, and humor to our partnership. I am proud and honored to be your friend. And thank you, too, Courtney, for your hospitality, your gallettes, and the example you set for so many, myself included.

Thanks also go to my friends Jane Slotin and Jane Wettach, who have made my life richer for decades. Thank you to my son, Max, for keeping me on my toes and amazing me on a regular basis. And deepest thanks to my husband, Andy, who keeps me going with his expansive thinking, unfailing encouragement, and just the right brand of humor. You know I couldn't do it without you, and even if I could, it wouldn't be nearly as much fun.

Finally, my gratitude goes to all of the mothers—and fathers, husbands, and wives—whose wisdom and experiences have contributed to this book. I respect and appreciate your strength, your courage, your resilience, and your warrior spirits—not to mention your children or spouses, and all who serve.

Sources/References

The research supporting "From Ballet Slippers to Combat Boots" and "The Sneaky Bastard" can be found in the following virtual locations:

FROM BALLET SLIPPERS TO COMBAT BOOTS

"Women, Trauma, and PTSD," US Department of Veterans Affairs, National Center for PTSD, http://www.ptsd.va.gov/public/PTSD-overview/women/women-trauma-and-ptsd.asp.

Christopher Munsey, "Women and War: Researchers Find a Link Between Sexual Trauma and Post-deployment PTSD, but Signs of Resilience, Too," *Monitor on Psychology* 40, no. 8 (September 2009), p. 32, http://www.apa.org/monitor/2009/09/women-war.aspx.

Steve Tokar, "Almost One Third of Iraq/Afghanistan Women Veterans with PTSD Report Military Sexual Trauma, Researchers Find," University of California, San Francisco, National Center of Excellence in Women's Health, September 14, 2011, http://www.coe.ucsf.edu/coe/research/ptsd-sexualtrauma.html.

Laura Kasinoff, "Women, War, and PTSD," *Washington Monthly*, November/December 2013, http://www.washingtonmonthly.com/magazine/november_december_2013/features/women_war_and_ptsd047354.php?page=all.

THE SNEAKY BASTARD

Moni Basu, "Why Suicide Rate Among Veterans May Be More Than 22 a Day," CNN, November 14, 2013, http://www.cnn.com/2013/09/21/us/22-veteran-suicides-a-day/.

"VA Issues New Report on Suicide Data," February 13, 2013, US Department of Veterans Affairs, http://www.va.gov/opa/pressrel/pressrelease.cfm?id=2427.

Janet Kemp and Robert Bossart, "Suicide Data Report, 2012," Department of Veterans Affairs, Mental Health Services, Suicide Prevention Program, http://www.va.gov/opa/docsSuicide-Data-Report-2012-final.pdf.

"Women, Trauma, and PTSD," US Department of Veterans Affairs, National Center for PTSD, http://www.ptsd.va.gov/public/PTSD-overview/women/women-trauma-and-ptsd.asp.

Veterans and PTSD, "Veterans Statistics: PTSD, Depression, TBI, Suicide," http://www.veteransandptsd.com/PTSD-statistics.html.

"First Lady Michelle Obama Announces Major Coordinated Effort by America's Academic Institutions to Combat PTSD & TBI," The White House, January 11, 2012, http://www.whitehouse.gov/the-press-office/2012/01/11/first-lady-michelle-obama-announces-major-coordinated-effort-americas-ac.

Photo by Tonya Brye, Brye Photography

Elaine Lowry Brye grew up as an Army brat, married an Air Force pilot, and ultimately became a mom to four military officers, one each in the Army, Navy, Air Force, and Marine Corps. For the last fourteen years she has been mentoring parents as they make the adjustment to military-parent life through the USNA-Parents listserv and in other online forums. Her professional life has included a bachelor's degree in medical technology, a master's in business, training in Air Force ROTC, and certification as a science educator. In 2010–2011, she spent a year teaching in Kabul, Afghanistan, gaining her own experience in a war zone. But the role she is most proud of—besides "mom"—and which has taken her to the White House and to the stage of the Democratic National Convention, is that of dogged supporter of military families. She lives with her husband on a farm in Northeast Ohio.

Photo by Andy Satter

Nan Gatewood Satter is a writer and independent book editor. The daughter of a highly decorated Navy fighter pilot, she lives in New York's Hudson Valley with her husband and son.